INTEGRATING
PITTSBURGH
SPORTS

THE ASSOCIATION OF GENTLEMAN PITTSBURGH JOURNALISTS

FOREWORD BY SAMUEL W. BLACK

THE
History
PRESS

Published by The History Press
Charleston, SC
www.historypress.com

Front cover, top left: The 1932 Pittsburgh Crawfords. Courtesy of the Pittsburgh Pirates; *top right*: Jim Tucker. Courtesy of Duquesne University Athletics; *center*: Joe Greene. Courtesy of North Texas Athletics; *bottom left*: John Woodruff. Courtesy of the University of Pittsburgh Athletics; *bottom right*: Charles West. Courtesy of Washington & Jefferson College Athletics.
Back cover, top right: Al Oliver. Courtesy of the Pittsburgh Pirates; *center*: Dick Ricketts (*top*) and Dave Ricketts. Courtesy of Duquesne University Athletics; *bottom*: Roberto Clemente. Courtesy of the Pittsburgh Pirates.

First published 2023

Manufactured in the United States

ISBN 9781467152594

Library of Congress Control Number: 2022944971

To the heroes of integration in Pittsburgh.
Their efforts and struggles opened the door for so many who came behind them.

Hanging from the rafters of the Palumbo Center, the old arena that housed Duquesne basketball, are the retired jersey numbers of Sihugo Green (11) and Dick Ricketts (12). After leading the school to its lone national title in the 1955 National Invitation Tournament, the players set a record that has yet to be broken: the only back-to-back first overall selections in the NBA draft from the same school. *Courtesy of David Finoli.*

CONTENTS

CONTENTS

FOREWORD

Today, sports in Pittsburgh are largely integrated in terms of race, ethnicity, sex and class. It is easy to forget that the racial and gender integration of sports we see today has not always been the case. Nor was it an easy transition from segregated sports to the integration of the stadium, arena, field or pitch that we are so accustomed to today. Sports in the twentieth century was a major part of American social culture. The segregation that existed in our communities, schools, churches, businesses, colleges and politics existed in our sports as well. The integration of sports in Pittsburgh took place in the twentieth century and paralleled the growth of the African American community in the city at the time of the Great Migration.

Sports exploded in greater Pittsburgh after the turn of the twentieth century. The influx of African American migrants, mostly from the southern United States, and the immigration of Europeans provided athletes for Pittsburgh's playing fields. From 1900 to 1960, popular sports included baseball, basketball, football and boxing. Secondary sports were track and field, golf, soccer, tennis, bowling, gymnastics, swimming and cricket. Some sports were more popular with immigrants from both Europe and the Caribbean. But the heart of American sports of the twentieth century lay in baseball, basketball, football and boxing, followed by track and field. David Finoli and his colleagues have written a book that explores the integration of Pittsburgh sports and its impact on societal efforts to integrate and find racial harmony in America.

Sport has shown over time to be a weapon for social change and has often led the way to racial and gender integration. Conversely, it has also been the gatekeeper for racial discrimination and segregation, reflecting those issues in American society. Pittsburgh has experienced a great deal of success in its sporting history. Numerous teams and individuals have achieved championship status in professional and amateur sports. The city has also served as a popular place for boxing, the only major individual sport in the discussion. Baseball began as a recreational pastime during the Civil War and was played by whites and African Americans alike. Just four years after the end of the war in 1865, the first professional baseball team was founded. Professional baseball had a few instances of integration, but by 1884, when Moses Fleetwood Walker was denied a contract, baseball had begun an era of segregation that lasted until Jackie Robinson was signed by the Brooklyn Dodgers' minor league team in Montreal in 1945.

Between the end of Walker's career in 1884 and Robinson's signing in 1945, baseball in Pittsburgh was segregated. In 1887, the Pittsburgh Keystone Quartette became the first local African American team recognized as a professional club. From this point on, Pittsburgh would field professional Negro league and sandlot baseball teams, leading to the integration of the game in the 1940s. After Rube Foster formed the Negro National League in 1920, Pittsburgh went on to be the only city with two league teams. Future Hall of Famers Josh Gibson, Cool Papa Bell, Oscar Charleston, Judy Johnson, Jud Wilson, Satchel Paige, Smokey Joe Williams and others played for either the Homestead Grays, Pittsburgh Crawfords or both. The Grays and the Crawfords played integrated games against regional semipro teams and solidified a foundation for the love of baseball in the African American community. The teams would list future Hall of Famers on each roster, as well as Grays' manager Cum Posey.

Much like the Negro leagues, in the early years of basketball, African American teams played some integrated games against local clubs. Some of the earliest basketball teams were the Monticello Athletic Club, Scholastic Athletic Association, Delany Rifles and Leondi Big Five. They played against teams such as the Jewish Coffey Club and Second Story Morries. Minor examples of basketball integration existed across the country, but in Pittsburgh, it was limited to a few games. Two-sport star Cum Posey led the Monticello team and, in the 1920s, the Loendi Big Five to local and national prominence. These early basketball teams laid a foundation for the success at Duquesne University in the 1950s and played a part in the integration of basketball across the country. Local high school stars Chuck

Dudey Moore is lifted off the ground by his players as Duquesne captures the only national championship in the basketball program's history, winning the 1955 National Invitation Tournament. *Courtesy of Duquesne University Athletics.*

Cooper, Bill Nunn Jr., Dick Ricketts, Maurice Stokes and Jack Twyman held integrated games at local parks, including Mellon Park in Shadyside. Cooper and Nunn were teammates at Westinghouse High School and West Virginia State University before Cooper played for Duquesne and Nunn went to work for the *Pittsburgh Courier*; Twyman and Stokes played together at Mellon Park, then for the Cincinnati Royals in the NBA. Twyman and Stokes maintained their friendship after being taken in the 1955 NBA draft (Stokes in round 1; Twyman in round 2) by the Rochester Royals. Their friendship was illustrated after Stokes suffered paralysis due to a head injury during a game, and Twyman became his legal guardian and overseer of his medical care. The Rochester Royals had four Pittsburghers on their 1955 roster. Joining Stokes and Twyman were Dick Ricketts and Ed Fleming. The integrated Mellon Park pickup games translated to the professional ranks.

Football evolved from early 1900s sandlot teams throughout the city. Rob Ruck documented many of these teams, including the Delany Rifles. The sandlot seasons of football in the first fifty years of the twentieth century involved neighborhood teams that reflected the segregation of their communities. There were significant instances of integration in regional college football. Charlie "Pruner" West was a star player for Washington & Jefferson College (W&J) when it played California in the 1922 Rose Bowl. He integrated not only W&J but also the Rose Bowl, becoming the first African American to play in the Tournament of Roses game in Pasadena, California. In 1945, Connellsville native Jimmy Joe Robinson became the first African American on Pitt's football team. He was soon joined by Hazelwood's two-sport athlete Herb Douglass. Douglass became the first African American to score against Notre Dame. By 1955, Bobby Grier had joined the Pitt team and became the first African American to play in the Sugar Bowl. As college football teams increasingly integrated their squads, most major southern teams maintained segregated schools and football teams. The age of desegregation had begun slowly after the 1954 *Brown v. Board of Education* Supreme Court decision overturned *Plessy v. Ferguson*. It wasn't until the 1970s that southern colleges began to integrate and offer scholarships to African American football payers. Local high school football offers great examples of integrated teams. Braddock High School and Westinghouse High School dominated the Western Pennsylvania Interscholastic Athletic League (WPIAL) and City League in the decades following World War II.

Just two years before the W&J heroics in the Rose Bowl, the National Football League was formed. The NFL opened with integrated teams. From 1920 to 1933, the NFL had a number of African American players, including Hall of Famer Fritz Pollard. Within a decade, the Pittsburgh Pirates football team was organized by Art Rooney Sr. from the sandlot teams he oversaw. Integration didn't necessarily hit the Pirates right away. Legend has it that Gus Greenlee loaned the entry fee to Rooney for his NFL franchise. In 1933, the year the Pirates joined the NFL, they also signed Cecil, Pennsylvania native Ray Kemp. But after only three games, Kemp was cut by the team. Conflicting stories say that Kemp was placed on reserves and decided to quit, or that player-coach Jap Douds cut him because they played the same position. The NFL had just two African Americans in the league by the end of the 1933 season and then was all white until pro football integrated again in 1946.

Boxing, an ancient sport compared to the other three, had its moments of integration and segregation in America. There is some form of boxing, wrestling and martial arts in the history of most world cultures. Boxing in the twentieth century dealt with integration mainly because of the presence of good African American fighters who at times dominated their weight classes. Joe Gans was the first African American champion of the twentieth century, but his mastery of the lightweight division was overshadowed by the presence and legacy of heavyweight Jack Johnson. Johnson fought two Pittsburgh-area natives during his reign as champion. In 1909, he defeated New Castle's Tony Ross at the Duquesne Gardens in Oakland; in 1911, he beat Pittsburgh's Frank Moran in Paris, France. Integration existed at times in the fight game but less so when world championship belts were on the line. Pittsburgh has a deep and impressive history in boxing. The golden era of Pittsburgh boxing stretched from the 1920s, with middleweight champion Harry Greb, through the 1950s, featuring Fritzie Zivic, Billy Conn, Billy Soose, Los Angeles transplant and former light heavyweight champion John Henry Lewis and the uncrowned champion Charley Burley. During this golden era of Pittsburgh boxing, African American and white fighters faced each other all the time. Zivic climbed into the ring with some of the greatest fighters of all time, including Sugar Ray Robinson, Henry Armstrong, Jake LaMotta and crosstown rival Charley Burley. Segregation affected opportunities to fight for the title, but the color line in boxing was long a memory by the middle of the century.

—Samuel W Black

ACKNOWLEDGEMENTS

I've studied and researched these men most of my adult life. It started with a paper I wrote about the Negro leagues at Duquesne. I was inspired by the research conducted by Bill Ranier, my roommate at Duquesne. I am pleased to still call him a close friend and am honored to have worked with him on several books, including this one.

As I read more into the experiences of people like Josh Gibson, Oscar Charleston and Buck Leonard, to name a few, I felt both a sadness and an anger that came with the prejudice they went through and the fact that they never had the chance to play in the major leagues because of the color of their skin.

As I grew older, I began to research people in other sports who had to fight the same barriers of prejudice to take their rightful place among the game's elite. For many of them, their incredible stories developed in western Pennsylvania. They include Bobby Grier, Jimmy Joe Robinson, Charley Burley, Jackie Wilson, Harry Bobo, John Woodruff, Herb Douglas, Dick Ricketts, Sihugo Green and a man with whom I had the honor of cowriting his autobiography along with his son Chuck Cooper III: Chuck Cooper, a man I am proud to call my hero.

Of course, I can research and tell the stories of what these men went through. But I can never truly feel what they did or experience the bravery it took to not only become great athletes but also to do so with the barriers of prejudice that each faced and overcame to attain their level of success. We can tell their stories and honor their lives and experiences, as I do

Chuck Cooper III, the son of Hall of Famer Chuck Cooper, stands in front of the gymnasium in Wilkinsburg where Duquesne University forfeited a game against the University of Tennessee when the Volunteers' coach, John Mauer, refused to let his team take the court if the Dukes insisted on playing an African American player, Chuck Cooper. *Courtesy of Chuck Cooper III.*

in this book along with an exceptional group of writers, including Tom Rooney, Chris Fletcher, Samuel Black, Bill Ranier, Robert Healy III, Josh Taylor, Gary Kinn, Rich Boyer and Douglas Cavanaugh. We thank our families for the wonderful support through not only this endeavor but also all the others through our lives.

This is the sixth project we've partnered with The History Press on, and we couldn't ask for a more perfect publisher to work with, especially our acquisitions editor, Banks Smither, who has been with us on each book.

There are those who gave of their time to allow us to interview them, such as Sean Gibson, Chuck Cooper III, Stewart Johnson, Linda West Nickens and Rob Ruck.

We also more than appreciate and thank the wonderful people who donated pictures to the project, including E.J. Borghetti of the University of Pittsburgh; Jim Trdinich of the Pittsburgh Pirates, the athletic communication department at North Texas University and the University of Minnesota; and Dave Saba from Duquesne University.

Finally, we thank the men who are included in this book for fighting through the prejudices they endured to become the icons they are. We do what we can to honor their efforts and memories: we tell their stories.

INTRODUCTION

Integration of Pittsburgh sports happened largely because of love of the game and social contact. Integration was hard to come by, due to the lack of integrated communities that supported their teams and larger issues of racial segregation in the country. The few instances of early twentieth-century integration were the exception, not the rule. Social convention of racial segregation was strong. Almost every aspect of life in the city was affected by racial segregation. The school a person attended, the neighborhood they lived in, the job they held and even the places they went for recreation and entertainment were largely impacted by racial segregation. Sports served as a level playing field and, over time, was one of the cultural traditions that ushered in integration.

I

BASEBALL

1

A GREAT-GRANDSON BEARS JOSH GIBSON'S TORCH

By Tom Rooney

I t was on those two-hour drives on winding roads to and from Pittsburgh and Edinboro University that Sean Gibson enjoyed long discussions with the man he called "Dad" about Josh Gibson, the famous catcher for the Pittsburgh Crawfords and Homestead Grays. "Dad" was Sean's grandfather and the father figure in his life. "Dad" was also Josh Gibson Jr. He was determined that the memory of one of the greatest baseball players of any era and any league should never fade, even if Major League Baseball had denied the great slugger entry. And ferrying his grandson back and forth to college was a good way for Gibson Jr. to pass the time and, maybe, the torch.

"I was a criminology major and looking forward to a career in law enforcement," remembers Sean, president and CEO of the Josh Gibson Foundation. "I loved hearing the stories and since 'Dad' was a batboy for his father's team, he had a lot of them. I'm thinking he was gradually working me to get more involved with the foundation he had set up. But working for a nonprofit didn't look that profitable from a personal standpoint. I was skeptical," Sean says.

That reluctance dissipated rapidly when Sean Gibson had a Chantilly epiphany.

"I used to accompany 'Dad' to the baseball card signings that were really starting to get popular in the 1990s around the country," Sean says.

We were in the convention center in Chantilly, Virginia, and a guy and his young son came up to our table. First, I was blown away because almost everyone at this convention was white. I wrongly assumed only Black people cared about the Negro leagues. Anyway, this white guy and his young son came up to our table. The father says to his maybe six-year-old son, "Okay, tell the Gibson family here what you know about Josh." This little white kid rips off a string of facts and figures about Josh a mile long. I thought, wait, Black kids back home don't know anything about Josh Gibson and look at this kid. It was time to go to work!

Josh Gibson's life was a mix of triumph and tragedy. He hit mammoth home runs, and historical markers like the one installed in 2021 in Monessen, Pennsylvania, attest to that. He was a catcher on nine Negro league championship teams. In barnstorming exhibition games in the offseason against teams made up of white stars, he amazed, and more than

Arguably the greatest home-run hitter in the history of the game, Josh Gibson is shown in a Grays uniform. Unfortunately, he never had the opportunity to show his skills in a Major League Baseball uniform. Even without that opportunity, he is one of the great athletes in western Pennsylvania history. *Courtesy of the Pittsburgh Pirates.*

one opponent suggested he would be an immediate improvement at the position for all but a handful of National or American League teams, which were composed solely of white players.

But there seemed to be problems for Josh throughout his life. His son Josh Jr., who would start the foundation years later, and a twin sister, Helen, were born to their eighteen-year-old mom, Helen, but the difficult childbirth took her life. It was reported that Josh had wanted the doctors to save his wife's life at the expense of the twins, figuring they'd have a chance to have more children later. But it was too late. The event seemed to sour Gibson on life away from the diamond. He reportedly fell into deep bouts of drinking and depression.

Then, at the age of thirty-five, disabling headaches were misdiagnosed, and Josh Gibson died of an undetected brain tumor, ironically only months before Jackie Robinson broke the major league color line in 1946.

Between bouts of tragedy and sadness, there was absolute greatness from Josh Gibson. Many Caucasians called him the "Colored Babe Ruth." And in response, many people of color referred to Ruth as the "White Josh Gibson."

Born in 1911 in Buena Vista, Georgia, Josh Gibson moved with his family to Pittsburgh when he was twelve. His father, Mark, discovered that work was available in the steel mills, which didn't discriminate on color. (In fact, pictures from that era show factory workers leaving the mills. Even white workers looked like Black men in pictures from the times as they left the mills covered in soot.)

At age sixteen, playing third base for a team sponsored by a department store, Josh was discovered and recruited to play for the early version of the Pittsburgh Crawfords, one of two Negro Leagues teams in the area, along with the Homestead Grays. Gibson's legendary career spanned the next seventeen years, and his plaque at the National Baseball Hall of Fame notes: "Considered greatest slugger in Negro Baseball Leagues. Power hitting catcher who hit almost 800 home runs…in 17-year career…Negro League Batting Champion in 1936-38-42-43."

His place in the National Baseball Hall of Fame in Cooperstown took a long time to develop. The Hall only began admitting Negro league players in 1971, when Satchel Paige had the first singular honor for a Black player. That started a drip, drip, drip of Negro league players who followed Paige beginning the following year. The honor to follow up fell to Gibson in 1972, a bittersweet occasion twenty-five years after his last season and his very premature death. But it wasn't until 2021 that Major League Baseball accepted the individual stats of the Negro leaguers among its own, resulting in players like Gibson almost overnight populating high perches on the all-time category lists.

Josh Gibson's new official MLB stats include only the seventy or so regular-season Negro league games. Gibson played many more games each year in barnstorming exhibition matchups, some against white players. One of those white players was Art Rooney, a great athlete in his own right but better known as the founder of the NFL's Pittsburgh Steelers. "Greatest hitter I ever saw," Art was quoted as saying. Gibson played year-round, spending winters in Central America, where the Latin population did not differentiate themselves from Blacks. Gibson was a revered figure.

The same MLB system that barred Black players saw stars like Gibson in the barnstorming and winter ball sessions and would grudgingly admit those men could play. "Josh Gibson would be the starting catcher for all but a few of our teams," one executive was anonymously quoted as saying. Many white players working under the customary one-year contracts knew that the influx of Black players to the MLB would cost a lot of them their living.

The bat boy Josh Jr. had a dugout view of his dad's greatness. "I think my grandfather harbored a little guilt that he and his twin sister Helen survived their childbirth but their mom didn't," Sean Gibson remarked. "So, Josh Jr. dedicated all the time he could to promoting his legacy, all the while working a regular job and raising a family. He set up youth programs that not only taught baseball skills but also classroom tutoring and nutrition. And he was a Negro leagues player himself for a while. Josh may have been born a decade too early, because by the time Jackie Robinson got the chance to break the color line, Josh was already thirty-five and his abilities had diminished. He never got a chance to play and never even saw Jackie play in the Major Leagues, because he died the winter before all that."

Sean Gibson gave up a career in law enforcement and accepted the mantle from his grandfather to run the Josh Gibson Foundation. "It's not the best-paying job to run a foundation, but I do it for the two Josh Gibson figures in my life," Sean said. "Josh Jr. saw his dad make the Hall of Fame and now I got to see the acceptance of Negro leagues players as one of the recognized major leagues. My grandfather's shuttle service for me back and forth to Edinboro was a process to redirect my career, and it's been a pleasure and privilege to be the keeper of the flame."

2

INTEGRATION BY THE NUMBERS

THE HOMESTEAD GRAYS AND PITTSBURGH CRAWFORDS BECOME PART OF MAJOR LEAGUE HISTORY

By David Finoli

For the vast majority of Negro league players, integration was nothing more than a pipe dream reserved for the few who followed Jackie Robinson into Major League Baseball after he made his historic debut in 1947. For stars like Josh Gibson, Oscar Charleston, Judy Johnson and Buck Leonard, integration into the majors was an unattainable goal. While it wasn't the same as actually playing in the major leagues, integration took another form for 3,400 Negro League players on December 16, 2020, when Commissioner Rob Manfred announced that the Negro leagues would get official major league status. The statistics of those who played in the Negro National League I (1920–31), the Eastern Colored League (1923–28), the American Negro League (1929), the East-West League (1932), the Negro Southern League (1932), the Negro National League II (1933–48) and the Negro American League (1937–48) would soon appear in the record books next to those of their counterparts in Major League Baseball.

In an article on MLB.com the same day the announcement was made, Manfred proclaimed that this was long overdue and that "all of us who love baseball have long known that the Negro Leagues produced many of the game's best players, innovations and triumphs against the backdrop of injustice. We are now grateful to count the players of the Negro Leagues where they belong: as Major Leaguers within the official historical record."

Left: Buck Leonard is one of the most gifted players to come out of the Negro leagues. A member of the Homestead Grays for fourteen seasons, Leonard was a powerful hitter who finished his career with a .345 average and a 1.042 OPS, including two batting titles. He hit .420 in 1938. *Courtesy of the Pittsburgh Pirates*.

Right: The Homestead Grays' Oscar Charleston was one of the greatest players in the history of not only the Negro leagues but also in all of baseball. Charleston played for both the Grays and Crawfords, compiling a .364 career batting average in eighteen seasons and a 1.063 OPS. *Courtesy of the Pittsburgh Pirates*.

In 1968, a special committee was formed by the commissioner at the time, William Eckart, to decide which leagues in the history of the game would be considered to have major league status alongside the American and National Leagues. It was decided that the American Association, the Union Association, the Players League and the Federal League would receive this status. The Negro leagues weren't considered, at the time, more so because its records were incomplete. Over the years, through the incredible research by the likes of Larry Lester, Lawrence Hogan, James Riley and John Holway, to name a few, the official Negro league statistics are just about complete, and their inclusion as major league statistics is deserved.

Above: This pennant commemorates the 1935 Pittsburgh Crawfords, considered one of the greatest Negro league teams ever assembled. *Courtesy of David Finoli.*

Left: The historical marker placed where Greenlee Field used to stand. Built by Pittsburgh Crawfords owner Gus Greenlee, the facility housed the famed Crawford teams in the mid-1930s, some of the greatest squads ever assembled. It was razed in 1938 after the team fell on hard financial times to make way for affordable housing. *Courtesy of Sean Gibson.*

For baseball fans in Pittsburgh, it means that some of the greatest players the game has known, representing the Homestead Grays and Pittsburgh Crawfords, now stand next to those from the other major league teams in the Steel City, namely the Alleghenys, Stogies, Burghers, Rebels and Pirates.

Even though this was a designation that should have happened years earlier, especially when the Negro league stats were being pulled together in the early part of the twenty-first century, it has finally become a reality. In this chapter, we will look at Pittsburgh's Negro league teams by the numbers, in the official context laid out by Major League Baseball, using only the leagues that count toward those numbers. (The 1931 Grays, considered one of the greatest Negro league teams of all time, was an independent team that season and will not be listed in this section.)

PITTSBURGH KEYSTONES

YEAR: 1922
LEAGUE: Negro National League
ALL-TIME RECORD: 14-24-2 (.368)
PENNANTS: 0
NEGRO LEAGUE WORLD SERIES CHAMPIONSHIPS: 0
HALL OF FAMERS: 0

FRANCHISE LEADERS:

Hitting			Pitching		
Category	Player	Total	Category	Player	Total
Games	Bull Barbour	41	Games	Bill McCall	23
At Bats	Gerard Williams	157	Wins	Bill McCall	5
Runs	Willie Gray	36	Saves	Bill McCall	1
Hits	Willie Gray	52	Losses	Charles Corbett	8
Doubles	Oscar Owens	14	Innings Pitched	Charles Corbett	118
Triples	Willie Gray	3	Strikeouts	Bill McCall	62
Home Runs	Oscar Owens	5	Starts	Charles Corbett	16
RBIs	Oscar Owens	28	Complete Games	Charles Corbett	9
Stolen Bases	Willie Gray	7	Shutouts	Charles Corbett	1
Batting Average	Oscar Owens	.405	Walks	Charles Corbett	37
Slugging %	Oscar Owens	.685	Hits	Charles Corbett	166
On-base %	Oscar Owens	.463	ERA	Bill McCall	5.62
OPS	Oscar Owens	1.148	Winning %	Dizzy Dismukes	.500

HOMESTEAD GRAYS

YEARS: 1929, 1932–33, 1935–48
LEAGUES: American Negro League, East-West League, Negro National League
ALL-TIME RECORD: 629-377-30 (.625)
PENNANTS: 1937, 1938, 1939, 1940, 1941, 1942, 1943, 1944, 1945, 1948
NEGRO LEAGUE WORLD SERIES CHAMPIONSHIPS: 1943, 1944, 1948
HALL OF FAMERS: Buck Leonard, Josh Gibson, Cool Papa Bell, Judy Johnson, Oscar Charleston, Ray Dandridge, Leon Day, Willie Wells, Joe Williams, Jud Wilson, Cum Posey and Ray Brown

FRANCHISE LEADERS:

Hitting			Pitching		
Category	Player	Total	Category	Player	Total
Games	Jerry Benjamin	608	Games	Ray Brown	194
At Bats	Jerry Benjamin	2470	Wins	Ray Brown	113
Runs	Buck Leonard	534	Saves	Ray Brown	13
Hits	Jerry Benjamin	743	Losses	Ray Brown	36
Doubles	Buck Leonard	137	Innings Pitched	Ray Brown	1,317.1
Triples	Buck Leonard	46	Strikeouts	Ray Brown	590
Home Runs	Josh Gibson	104	Starts	Ray Brown	137
RBIs	Buck Leonard	550	Complete Games	Ray Brown	123
Stolen Bases	Jerry Benjamin	93	Shutouts	Ray Brown	16
Batting Average	Josh Gibson	.379	Walks	Ray Brown	337
Slugging %	Josh Gibson	.732	Hits	Ray Brown	1245
On-base %	Josh Gibson	.470	ERA	Ray Brown	3.01
OPS	Josh Gibson	1.203	Winning %	Ray Brown	.758

PITTSBURGH CRAWFORDS

YEARS: 1933–38 (in Pittsburgh), 1933–40 (includes three years in Toledo/Indianapolis)

LEAGUES: Negro National League II, Negro American League

ALL-TIME RECORD: 233-170-13 (.576) (in Pittsburgh), 252-204-15 (.553) (includes three years in Toledo/Indianapolis)

PENNANTS: 1933, 1934, 1935, 1936

WORLD SERIES CHAMPIONSHIPS: 0

HALL OF FAMERS: Satchel Paige, Josh Gibson, Cool Papa Bell, Judy Johnson, Oscar Charleston, Bill Foster, Jud Wilson and Biz Mackey

FRANCHISE LEADERS:

Hitting			Pitching		
Category	Player	Total	Category	Player	Total
Games	Chester Williams	278	Games	Leroy Matlock	67
At Bats	Chester Williams	1009	Wins	Leroy Matlock	32
Runs	Cool Papa Bell	230	Saves	Bert Hunter/ Theolic Smith	3
Hits	Cool Papa Bell	307	Losses	Harry Kincannon	19
Doubles	Josh Gibson/ Judy Johnson	52	Innings Pitched	Leroy Matlock	462
Triples	Josh Gibson	19	Strikeouts	Satchel Paige	301
Home Runs	Josh Gibson	61	Starts	Leroy Matlock	53
RBIs	Josh Gibson	256	Complete Games	Leroy Matlock	33
Stolen Bases	Cool Papa Bell	49	Shutouts	Satchel Paige	7
Batting Average	Josh Gibson	.365	Walks	Bill Harvey	125
Slugging %	Josh Gibson	.698	Hits	Leroy Matlock	456
On-base %	Josh Gibson	.437	ERA	Satchel Paige	2.16
OPS	Josh Gibson	1.135	Winning %	Satchel Paige	.714

Because Negro league seasons were much shorter than those of the major leagues, there were few if any changes to the all-time career statistical list. Most Negro league players did not have sufficient career at bats or innings pitched to qualify. But there were massive changes among the single-season leaders. Below is a list of some Homestead and Pittsburgh players who now find themselves among baseball's top fifty all-time leaders.

SINGLE-SEASON LEADERS:

Category	Place	Name	Year	Number
Hitters				
On-base %	3	Josh Gibson	1943	.560
	28	Josh Gibson	1937	.500
	28	Buck Leonard	1938	.500
	43	Josh Gibson	1939	.492
Batting Average	2	Josh Gibson	1943	.465
	22	Buck Leonard	1938	.420
	26	Josh Gibson	1937	.417
Slugging %	1	Josh Gibson	1937	.974
	4	Josh Gibson	1939	.823
	12	Josh Gibson	1936	.782
	14	Buck Leonard	1939	.780
	24	Josh Gibson	1933	.744
	25	Buck Leonard	1938	.740
	36	Buck Leonard	1937	.730
	43	Josh Gibson	1938	.721
OPS (on-base + slugging %)	1	Josh Gibson	1937	1.474
	2	Josh Gibson	1943	1.427
	11	Josh Gibson	1939	1.315
	16	Buck Leonard	1939	1.264
	17	Josh Gibson	1936	1.261
	25	Buck Leonard	1938	1.240
	43	Buck Leonard	1937	1.191
	44	Josh Gibson	1938	1.188

Category	Place	Name	Year	Number
	45	Josh Gibson	1933	1.186
Pitchers				
Winning %	1	Ray Brown	1938	1.000
	1	Leroy Matlock	1935	1.000
	33	Ray Brown	1944	.917
	41	Ray Brown	1940	.889
WHIP (walks + hits per inning pitched)	17	Satchel Paige	1933	0.826

CAREER LEADERS

Category	Place	Name	Number
Hitters			
OPS	4	Oscar Charleston	1.063
Batting Average	2	Oscar Charleston	.364
Slugging %	6	Oscar Charleston	.615
On-base %	5	Oscar Charleston	.449
Pitchers			
Winning %	2	Ray Brown	.731

3

IN THE BEGINNING

THE PIRATES' FORGOTTEN FIRST PLAYER OF COLOR, CARLOS BERNIER

By David Finoli

Carlos Bernier never had the chance to play with Roberto Clemente in professional baseball, but his short career with the Pirates, while relatively unknown by most Pirate fans, nonetheless was historic. It's almost as if he was cheated in his place in franchise history on two fronts.

The majority of Pirate fans believe that Roberto Clemente was the first Latin American to play for the team, and some think that Curt Roberts was the first player of color to wear the Pittsburgh uniform. In both cases, they are wrong. While Clemente certainly had the most distinguished career a Latin American Pirate has ever had, and Roberts was the first African American to appear in a game for the team, the honor of the first Latin American Pirate and first player of color for the franchise is one man: Carlos Bernier. He was a player of immense talent but one who had a troubled past and is largely forgotten in Pittsburgh history.

Born on January 28, 1927, in Juana Díaz, Puerto Rico, Bernier started his career in the independent Mandak League. In 1948, he joined Jackie Robinson, Larry Doby and Hank Thompson as organized baseball's only Black players when he joined the Port Chester Clippers of the Class B Colonial League. While the Clippers were part of the St. Louis Browns organization, his contract was owned by the Clippers. Unlike Robinson, who promised Dodgers general manager Branch Rickey that he would ignore racial taunts early in his career, Bernier was aggressive toward those who came after him.

Branch Rickey (at bottom in a suit) talks to his players at spring training. Rickey was not only responsible for signing Jackie Robinson while with Brooklyn, but he also signed Carlos Bernier and Curt Roberts and selected Roberto Clemente in the Rule 5 draft. *Courtesy of the Pittsburgh Pirates.*

The Juana Díaz native was an immensely talented player who unfortunately become known more for a fiery temper than for what he did on the field. According to his biography on the Society of American Baseball Research website, written by Charles F. Faber, Bernier was hit in the head while with Port Chester, and this caused painful headaches throughout his life, headaches that many blamed for his troublesome temper, which cost him a more successful career.

He eventually was sent to Indianapolis in the American Association before being sent back to Bristol in the Colonial League. He abandoned his attempt at switch-hitting. Carlos had a phenomenal season with the Owls, hitting .336.

The man nicknamed "The Comet" headed for a successful stint with St. Jean in the Provincial League after the Colonial folded, moving to Tampa in the Florida International League before jumping to the Pacific Coast League's Hollywood Stars, where he was named rookie of the year in 1952 after helping the Stars to the crown.

It had been an impressive five minor league seasons for the twenty-six-year-old, and he would get a shot at the majors in 1953 when he made the Pirates' roster, becoming the first player of color to debut with the club.

As spring training went on that season, Carlos was being recognized as a talent who could help turn around a franchise that had been in the doldrums since its surprising second-place finish in 1948. The *Pittsburgh Press* pointed out in its team preview on April 15 that Bernier had the one attribute that Rickey, who was now the Pirates' GM, loved: speed. The paper pointed out that he had 301 stolen bases in his minor league career to that point, averaging 63 a year. He was also a solid hitter.

The 1953 Pirates weren't a talented team but had many notable players. There was Ralph Kiner, the star who had held out in the spring and eventually found his way to the Cubs when Rickey traded him midseason. There was a light-hitting catcher who eventually became a broadcasting icon, Joe Garagiola. Other players of note were Vic Janowicz, the Heisman Trophy winner out of Ohio State, and the O'Brien twins, Eddie and Johnny, better known as college basketball stars with the University of Seattle.

In going through the newspapers of the time, not much was made about the color of Bernier's skin as he made his major league debut in the team's sixth game of the season. In that game, he pinch-hit for pitcher Paul LaPalme in the eighth inning. He was hit by a Jim Hearn pitch with the bases loaded, knocking in the first run of his major league career. He eventually scored his initial run later in the inning on a Kiner sacrifice fly.

It was a fine debut that led to his first start a day later against the Giants, when he was hitless in four at bats. By the end of the month, he had gone on a three-game tear against the Cubs and Reds at Forbes Field that got him the starting position full-time and some notoriety. In the first game against the Cubs on April 30 in front of just 2,930 people, he tripled in the sixth inning then knocked in the tying run in the eighth with a single that a turned into a double with his hustle. The *Pittsburgh Post-Gazette* exclaimed that he had won the center field job with an incredible catch in the ninth to save reliever Elroy Face and the Bucs in a 4–2 victory.

The next day, they beat the Reds, 8–3, with Carlos doubling and also showing his speed in the eighth when he went from first base to second on a wild pitch and then headed to third as catcher Hank Foiles tossed the ball into the outfield. Berner never stopped running and headed home, scoring on a throwing error from the outfield. The two games would be a precursor to his greatest performance with the Bucs, the day he set a major league record that still stands today.

The Bucs crushed the Reds again, this time 12–4, as Bernier was the star. Charles Doyle of the *Pittsburgh Sun-Telegraph* called Carlos "Puerto Rico's gift to Pittsburgh" that afternoon. He hit two triples that traveled four hundred feet each early on, one going to the flagpole in center on the fly and one hitting the gate in right center to go with a single. He then came up in the seventh. He walloped the ball to dead center and ended up at third base. He had tied the modern major league mark of three triples in one game. The record, while equaled, has never been bettered.

It was the high-water mark for the Latin star, whose season average stood at .385 after his remarkable performance. He started tumbling after that and by May 20 had dropped below .300, eventually losing his starting job in center. Bernier had some good moments the rest of the season, including on May 24, when he hit his first major league home run, against the Giants at Forbes in an 11–3 defeat, smacking the ball into the bullpen at Greenberg Gardens (which by now had been renamed Kiner's Korner) off the massive scoreboard. But his stats continued to falter as the season came to an end. Bernier finished the season hitting only .213. While he easily led the team with 15 stolen bases, he was caught stealing 14 times.

The next year, he was sent back to Hollywood after the Bucs spring training, where he started a violent melee against San Francisco that prompted the Pacific Coast League (PCL) commissioner to suspend him indefinitely.

Bernier never made the majors again, and while he had a successful career in the PCL that saw him inducted into the circuit's Hall of Fame in 2004, his career was marred by his many outbursts. Unfortunately, he eventually became homeless and died by suicide in 1989 in a garage in his hometown.

Despite the tragic way his life ended and the battles with his temper that outlined his career, Bernier deserves his spot in Pirate history as the man who broke the color line for the team and for that phenomenal day on May 2 at Forbes Field, where he showed his potential in a great career that could have been.

4

CURT ROBERTS

THE FIRST PITTSBURGH PIRATES AFRICAN AMERICAN PLAYER

By Bill Ranier

One year after the Pittsburgh Pirates debuted minority players by promoting Puerto Rican outfielders Carlos Bernier and Luis Márquez to the major league club, second baseman Curt Roberts became the first African American to play for the team. Like Márquez, Roberts's pedigree included time in the Negro leagues, but unlike Márquez, who had spent time with the Homestead Grays in the postwar 1940s, Roberts had not played for a Pittsburgh-based team prior to opening the 1954 season in the Steel City.

Roberts's journey to Pittsburgh began in Richland, Texas, where he was born in 1929. His family moved to Oakland, California, when Curt was a child, and he attended McClymonds High School, which became noteworthy for its stellar sports alumni, including baseball Hall of Famer Frank Robinson, all-stars Vada Pinson and Curt Flood and basketball great Bill Russell. Roberts graduated in 1947. Shortly afterward, he joined the Negro leagues' Kansas City Monarchs, the team Jackie Robinson played for prior to being signed by the Brooklyn Dodgers. Roberts hit .352 with a .936 OPS in 19 games that summer. He split his time between shortstop and second base. His second season was not as successful, as Roberts's hitting tailed off to .244 with only 11 extra-base hits in 46 games. Roberts did not possess an especially strong arm, so he became primarily a second baseman at this point. Following his time in the Negro leagues, Roberts was signed by the Denver Bears, an affiliate of the Boston Braves at the time. The Bears' manager was Andy Cohen, himself a former second baseman who had played with the New York Giants. Cohen worked with Roberts to improve the young man's defense.

In 1952, Denver became affiliated with the Pirates. Branch Rickey, the man who had signed Robinson for the Dodgers and brought him to the white major leagues in 1947, was now running the Pittsburgh ballclub. Rickey paid the Braves $10,000 in the hopes that Roberts might bolster the team's admittedly weak farm system. Cohen remained in Denver and further schooled Roberts in the art of playing second base. Roberts became proficient at the position. Still, questions remained about his hitting, as even in the 1950s, Denver was known as a hitter's haven. Roberts's averages ranged between .280 and .291 during his three years in the Mile High City, but in his final year, he added 46 extra-base hits, including 12 home runs. This earned him a chance to make Pittsburgh's roster in 1954.

By that time, it had been seven years since Jackie Robinson had broken the color barrier, and there was a movement in the local Black community for the Pirates to bring an African American player to Pittsburgh. As no player had distinguished himself at second in 1953, the door was open. Roberts won the job.

The opportunity for an African American was certainly overdue, and with the Pirates having been a National League doormat for the first four years of the decade, many fans hoped that the Bucs had come up with another Robinson. Roberts was known for his even temper, a quality Rickey valued. The general manager realized that Roberts would have to deal with the prejudices that were a terrible norm in the 1950s. Roberts would not be able to room with teammates on the road and would face restrictions in many Big League cities. However, according to Roberts's teammate Frank Thomas in his autobiography *Kiss It Goodbye: The Frank Thomas Story*, the other Pittsburgh players accepted Curt as a member of the club. "I never saw any mistreatment of Curt by Pirate fans or players," Thomas wrote. Bobby Bragan, who managed Roberts in both the major and minor leagues, was interviewed in 2002 for *The Pittsburgh Pirates Encyclopedia* and remembered Roberts as "a gentleman."

Second baseman Roberts led off for the Pirates in their April 13 opener and tripled in his first at bat. He held his regular job for the season and received positive reviews for his glove work. Although modern defensive metrics aren't particularly kind, Thomas remembered Roberts as "pretty good defensively." But Roberts did not provide the type of offense

Pittsburghers hoped for, batting .232 with only 1 home run. He did walk more times (55) than he struck out (49), but his on-base percentage was still just .306, and his slugging percentage was .324. Roberts also did not mirror the aggressive Robinson on the basepaths, stealing only 6 bases during the season. Still, Pirate management believed he had shown enough to be given another chance in 1955, but he opened the season with just 2 hits in 17 at bats and was sent down to AAA Hollywood. There, Roberts thrived, hitting an impressive .321 with 8 home runs and 17 stolen bases. This led to Curt being given another shot with the Pirates in 1956, but again he struggled, batting just .177 in 62 at bats before again being optioned to Hollywood. On June 23, he was traded to the Kansas City A's with Jack McMahan for another struggling second baseman, Spook Jacobs. From there, Roberts played AAA ball for the Yankees and Dodgers before finishing his professional career with a season for the White Sox AA affiliate in Lynchburg before retiring at the age of thirty-four. Despite several strong seasons in the minors (Roberts hit .291 or better four times), he never again appeared in a major league game.

Pie Traynor, the Pirates' Hall of Fame third baseman who later managed and scouted for the club, felt that part of the problem was that Roberts spent most of his minor league career playing in the Pacific Coast League, where high batting and slugging averages are common, particularly in Denver. While he was part of the Yankees' system, Roberts again found himself playing in Denver, where Traynor noted that the high altitude made throwing curve balls difficult. Because of this, Traynor felt Roberts struggled against curve balls in the majors. A look at Denver's players during this time seems to prove Traynor's hypothesis. The only position player who played for the Bears between 1951 and 1953 who had a significant offensive career was Billy Bruton, who became a solid offensive contributor for the Braves and Tigers, but even he was better known for his defense and speed on the bases than for overwhelming numbers with the bat. The only teammate who contributed offensively to a parent club from Roberts' years when Denver was a Yankee farm club was Johnny Blanchard, who, aside from an impressive year as a part-time player during the expansion season of 1961, totaled 46 home runs and a .222 batting average in his major league career.

Roberts's life ended tragically in 1969, when he was hit by a car while changing a tire along an Oakland, California freeway. While his on-field statistics were not the calling card of legends such as Robinson and other trailblazing African American ballplayers, Roberts deserves to be remembered and honored for being one of the athletes who helped break down barriers in Pittsburgh. Although his time playing alongside Roberto Clemente was limited, it has been said that Roberts, who spoke Spanish, provided counsel to the future star. That contribution alone may have helped lead to many Pirate wins long after Curt's time in Pittsburgh had ended.

5

ELEMENTS OF STYLE

ROBERTO CLEMENTE WAS HEROIC ON AND OFF THE FIELD

By Chris Fletcher

Honus Wagner may have been the best Pittsburgh Pirate of all time, but Roberto Clemente was the most important player to ever don a Bucco uniform. Fifty years after his death, he remains the face of the franchise. He is also still my favorite athlete, a title he's unlikely to ever cede.

There's the baseball Clemente and the off-the-diamond Clemente—and both have left an indelible mark on me and on the sport. On the field, he was the first baseball player from Latin America to collect three thousand hits. He earned four batting titles, twelve Gold Gloves, fifteen All-Star Game selections, one Most Valuable Player Award and a Hall of Fame induction. Off the diamond, he was a humanitarian, a spokesman for racial equality and a fighter for social and economic justice. There are more streets, schools, hospitals, fields and parks named after him than for any other athlete—even more than most presidents. There's even a Roberto Clemente Park in rival city Philadelphia.

There is something about Clemente that has captured the imagination of baseball fans and non-fans alike. Former commissioner Bowie Kuhn referred to it as "a touch of royalty." Filmmaker and author John Sayles was even more effusive in his praise. "I never thought about being a writer as I grew up. A writer wasn't something I wanted to be. An outfielder was something to be. Most of what I know about style I learned from Roberto Clemente."

In the 1950s, there was a rule that if a player was given a bonus of $6,000 or more, they had to be on a major league roster for two years or else be subject to the Rule 5 draft. The Dodgers signed Roberto Clemente and gave him a $10,000 bonus, then tried to hide him in their Montreal AAA team. The maneuver failed, and the Bucs made Clemente perhaps the greatest Rule 5 selection in the history of the game. *Courtesy of the Pittsburgh Pirates.*

When I was growing up in Pittsburgh in the 1960s, Clemente was my first baseball hero. Like Sayles, I enrolled in the Roberto Clemente School of Style. I imitated his stretching of the neck before taking my cuts. At ten, I mimicked every move and gesture of a player whose list of chronic maladies was mocked in *Sports Illustrated* and by his critics. Yet when it came time to play, he was the most complete baseball player of my youth.

Even today, when I close my eyes, I can picture the basket catches, the gazelle-like stride going from first to third, his batting helmet ejected about halfway to second. I remember the laser throws from deep right. I can see him bashing line drives, even breaking baseball norms by hitting off the wrong foot. He was a beautiful athlete to watch.

I wonder how different my baseball fandom would have been had Roberto not played here. It could have happened, thanks to Rule 5, an obscure baseball decree that rarely had any impact. In 1954, the Brooklyn Dodgers signed Clemente to a contract with a reported salary of $5,000, plus a signing bonus of $10,000. Rule 5 said that any player who signed for more than $4,000 had to be kept on the major league roster, or that player could be lost in an offseason draft.

The Dodgers tried to hide Clemente in Montreal, giving him a spot on the Royals in the International League and not playing him regularly, hoping to conceal his talent. Even though he struggled much of the season, the Pirates saw something in the young outfielder from Puerto Rico and snatched him up in the Rule 5 draft. By 1955, he was staring for the Bucs.

As a Pirate, Clemente toiled in relative obscurity, away from the bright lights of the bigger cities, where his fame could have been on par with Willie Mays or Mickey Mantle. Can you imagine Clemente playing in New York and then later in Los Angeles, two huge markets with large Puerto Rican populations? With his movie-star good looks, he could have been a cinematic idol off the field. Or maybe not. When asked by director Gene Saks to play a bit role in his movie *The Odd Couple*, Clemente refused, because the script called for him to hit into a triple play. Instead, that part went to Bill Mazeroski.

In Pittsburgh, Clemente was a star, but he had to deal with issues of racism as well as an often tempestuous relationship with the local media. First, they wanted to Anglicize his name—Bob Clemente was more approachable. Then they quoted him phonetically. "I heet dee ball." No other player on the team had to deal with that. Clemente once remarked that the press treatment he received because of his Latin culture and skin color made him feel like a "double nigger." It also may have planted the seeds of activism that he would later sow.

He welcomed fellow Latins to baseball and helped the Pirates find some of the best talent in that area. Manny Sanguillen, Rennie Stennett, Matty Alou and later Tony Pena, Omar Moreno and Bobby Bonilla all starred with the team.

The 1971 World Series, where he made the sport take notice of what we in Pittsburgh already knew, is my greatest moment as a fan. Clemente carried the Bucs to a title. I can still see the locker room interview, where he asked interviewer Bob Prince if it would be ok to send a message to his parents in Spanish. Roughly translated, he said, "On this, the proudest day of my life, I ask your blessings."

A little over a year later I experienced one of the saddest parts of my childhood. I woke up on January 1, 1973, to find my hero had perished on a mercy mission, personally bringing supplies to victims of a devastating earthquake so that their own government wouldn't poach them.

Part of me never got over his death. Baseball sought to honor his sacrifice, first by waiving the mandatory five years after retirement for enshrinement in Cooperstown. Then MLB named its humanitarian award after him. Just this past year, the league announced that each player who won the award would be able to wear Clemente's no. 21 on the back of their cap for the remainder of their careers.

Players from Latin America still hold Clemente in the highest regard, with many choosing 21 as their number. There is a movement in baseball, long overdue in my opinion, to retire the number across all of the sport, joining Jackie Robinson, who broke racial barriers, in that honor.

Personally, when I found out that I was going to have a son, I lobbied hard to name him Roberto. Roberto Fletcher kind of rolls off the tongue, I thought. His mother didn't share that thought, but through compromise we settled on Roberto as a middle name. Dylan Roberto still has a nice ring to it.

6

.414

CLEMENTE AND THE 1971 WORLD SERIES

By Rich Boyer

Pitch me outside, I will hit .400. Pitch me inside and you will not find the ball.
—Roberto Clemente

It ain't bragging if you can do it.
—Dizzy Dean

T he first pitch was high for ball one. The second pitch looked like another ball, but Bob Robertson fouled it off to make the count 1-1. Willie Stargell had walked on four straight pitches and stood at first base. Roberto Clemente led off second base, frantically trying to call time out after opening the inning by hustling down the baseline on a check swing, causing Mike Cuellar to hurry his throw, pulling Boog Powell off the bag. With Cuellar struggling, Clemente saw the bunt sign that Robertson missed and, unheeded, was trying to right the wrong. But I don't want to get ahead of myself.

In a World Series that included four 20-game winners, the 1971 home run champion, eight future Hall of Famers, seven Gold Glove winners, five MVPs and, ironically, two Roberto Clemente Award winners, Clemente used his voice, legs, arm and bat to outshine them all. Through 98 total pitches, 92 of which were supplied by 20-game winners, he had 12 hits, including 2 home runs, and hit 26 of them to center and right field. Yes, the Orioles pitched him outside and, yes, he hit .400. Not to get too deep into modern

Pirate great Roberto Clemente. After fighting through the injustice related to the color of his skin and his Latin American heritage, Clemente became a leader of the team in the late 1960s. In 1971, he led the franchise to its fourth World Series title, hitting .414 in his MVP performance in the Fall Classic. *Courtesy of the Pittsburgh Pirates.*

statistics, but Clemente's "win probability added for an offensive player" was a sterling .43. The closest Pirate was Manny Sanguillén, who tried to replace the "Great One" after his death in 1973, at .27. The closest Oriole was Don Buford at .09. He absolutely blew them all away. As he collected his MVP award for the World Series, he became a GOAT, way before someone by the name of Brady. Jim Palmer said about the 1971 World Series, "It was almost a fitting eulogy for him."

GAME 1: SATURDAY, OCTOBER 9, 1971
ATTENDANCE: 53,229
MEMORIAL STADIUM

Nobody does anything better than me in baseball.
—Roberto Clemente before the 1971 World Series

Coming off a 13-game winning streak, Dave McNally opened the first game of the World Series as the first 20-game winner to pitch to Clemente. Despite missing six weeks in late July and early August with a "sore arm," McNally still was able to lead his team with 21 wins. In his first at bat, Clemente saw an outside strike and did not wait any longer to extend his World Series hitting streak (which he had started in the 1960 World Series, which featured the historic Pirate comeback), stroking a double to center right on the next pitch. In the third inning, his second at bat lasted just three pitches with an outside ball and a strike that caught the outside corner. On the next pitch, an outside curveball, Clemente reached out and singled to center. In the fifth, his third at bat lasted three pitches, ending with a flyout to right. Roberto's last at bat in the opening game featured an inside brushback pitch and a line drive ball to second base. A great play by Davey Johnson notched the out. It was a 2-for-4 day totaling just 12 pitches for Clemente and a Pirate loss, 5–3. Clearly, Clemente was going to make things happen. After the game, he responded to rave reviews of McNally's performance: "I faced a lot of good pitchers. Any good one don't mean anything to me. Ask him what he thought about me. I get two hits off him, so I say we are even."

Cumulative Batting Line
R. Clemente

GP	AB	R	H	2B	3B	HR	RBI	BB	SO	AVG	PA	TB	Pitches
1	4	0	2	1	0	0	0	0	0	.500	4	3	12

GAME 2: MONDAY, OCTOBER 11, 1971
ATTENDANCE: 53,239
MEMORIAL STADIUM

Hall of Fame pitcher Jim Palmer, who faced Clemente only in this World Series, considered him and Rod Carew the two toughest hitters he ever faced. Even though the Orioles owned the second game, 11–3, it featured a classic Clemente performance with a single to center, a double to right, a lineout to deep right and a foul pop fly to right. In his last at bat, he reached base on an error by Mark Belanger at second base. He was on base when Richie Hebner hit a three-run home run, which accounted for all of the Pirate runs. On 16 total pitches in 5 at bats, Clemente put five balls to the center or right side of the field. But he was only getting warmed up.

Cumulative Batting Line
R. Clemente

GP	AB	R	H	2B	3B	HR	RBI	BB	SO	AVG	PA	TB	Pitches
2	9	1	4	2	0	0	0	0	0	.444	9	6	28

GAME 3: TUESDAY, OCTOBER 12, 1971
ATTENDANCE: 50,403
THREE RIVERS STADIUM

With the Orioles up two games to none, the series moved to two-year-old Three Rivers Stadium for a crucial game three. Starting pitcher Mike Cuellar was well known to—and not particularly well-liked by—Clemente. Just a year earlier, in winter ball, Clemente tried to manage Cuellar for the San Juan Senadores. Cuellar reported out of shape, chafed at Clemente's disciplinarian style and bolted the team after just a couple of games. It served to stoke the competitive fires, as if that was even needed. It took just 9 pitches for Roberto to put four balls in play, three of which were hit to the center or right side of the field. His first at bat featured three straight foul balls to right and a ground ball to second that scored Dave Cash for the first run of the game. That run scored only because Clemente hustled down the baseline and beat the double-play throw to first. His second at bat lasted only one pitch and ended with a rare bouncer to third base. In his third at bat, he looked at an outside breaking ball and then lined a single to center. Al Oliver, who was on first with a walk, drew the throw to third base while Clemente hustled toward second. He reached second standing up on a Brooks Robinson error. No runs were scored, but the table had been set for a series-turning seventh inning. After fouling off a fast ball, Clemente bounced a check swing to his favorite pupil and, with his hustle, reached first base on a bad throw from Cuellar. Clemente moved to second on a Willie

Stargell walk and was at second with the Pirates up, 2–1, trying to call a time out after he determined that Bob Robertson had missed a bunt sign. Some may say that this was the only mistake the Great One made in this World Series, but I say it was divine intervention. The time out was not taken, and Robertson powered the next pitch over the center-right-field wall for a 3-run homer and a 5–1 Pirate lead. The series and momentum had been turned on Clemente's legs on a day when he made solid contact just once. The best was yet to come.

Cumulative Batting Line
R. Clemente

GP	AB	R	H	2B	3B	HR	RBI	BB	SO	AVG	PA	TB	Pitches
3	13	2	5	2	0	0	1	0	0	.385	13	7	37

Game 4: Wednesday, October 13, 1971
Attendance: 51,378
Three Rivers Stadium

After notching their first win in the World Series, Clemente and the Pirates faced their fourth 20-game winner in a row while hosting the first night game in World Series history. Pat Dobson had his best season in the major leagues in 1971, sporting a 20-8 record and a 2.90 ERA and leading the Orioles with 18 complete games. He was throwing his curveball for strikes and fed Clemente a steady diet of them in his first three at bats. In the first, Dobson struck him out on six pitches, five of which were curves. This was only one of two strikeouts of Clemente in the seven-game series. By his second at bat, in the third inning, the Buccos were battling back from a 3–0 deficit at the hands of a wild and ineffective Luke Walker, who was replaced in the first by a lanky, wild, side-armed, twenty-one-year-old rookie, Bruce Kison. He was in the process of blanking the O's while hitting three batters. Clemente was not waiting around this time. He stroked a first pitch down the right-field line that was ruled foul and prompted a spirited argument from manager Danny Murtaugh. On his second pitch, he left no doubt how he felt with a line-drive single to right. On Clemente's third at bat, Dobson lobbed up three breaking balls. Clemente adjusted and hit the third pitch up the middle for a single. With the score tied, 3–3, Clemente stepped up against lefty Grant Jackson, who gave him almost nothing to hit, walking him on seven pitches and loading the bases. He hit a long foul ball to right on the only hittable pitch, with Murtaugh offering no resistance this time. By his fifth and final at bat, in the eighth against Eddie Watt, the Pirates were clinging to a 4–3 lead with closer Dave Giusti in charge. Clemente looked at strike one and then smoked a ball to deep short and somehow hustled his way to first for a single, beating Gold Glove shortstop Mark "The Blade" Belanger's throw. He ended a relatively quiet night with three hits in four at bats with the Pirates tying the series, 2-2.

Cumulative Batting Line
R. Clemente

GP	AB	R	H	2B	3B	HR	RBI	BB	SO	AVG	PA	TB	Pitches
4	17	2	8	2	0	0	1	1	1	.471	18	10	55

GAME 5: THURSDAY, OCTOBER 14, 1971
ATTENDANCE: 51,377
THREE RIVERS STADIUM

When Earl Weaver remarked, as the series moved to Pittsburgh, "We will have a tough time of it in Pittsburgh," he probably did not realize just how tough it would be. Game 5 featured a return of Dave "The Billings Bulldog" McNally against Nelson Briles, who had not pitched for a full two weeks. Briles, who had a propensity to fall down occasionally after a pitch, did not disappoint. He fell twice, while striking out Frank Robinson in the top of the fourth and while walking Elrod Hendricks in the fifth. Despite the on-the-mound gymnastics, Briles rose to the occasion, pitching a masterful 2-hit shutout and leading his team to a 4–0 win and a sweep of all three games at Three Rivers Stadium. Roberto Clemente did not disappoint either, knocking in the speedy Gene Clines with an RBI first-pitch single to center in the fifth, which ended Dave McNally's day. His first two shots at McNally ended with a two-strike liner to the right-field wall in the first and, staying on the right side, a two-strike bouncer to second. His last at bat against hard-throwing reliever Tom Dukes was a seven-pitch battle that included a called strike, two balls and three foul balls before a groundout to second base. During this last at bat, radio announcer Bill O'Donell ominously remarked that Clemente would hit .320 a year after his death.

Cumulative Batting Line
R. Clemente

GP	AB	R	H	2B	3B	HR	RBI	BB	SO	AVG	PA	TB	Pitches
5	21	2	9	2	0	0	2	1	1	.428	22	11	77

GAME 6: SATURDAY, OCTOBER 16, 1971
ATTENDANCE: 44,174
MEMORIAL STADIUM

Memorial Stadium is not a major league stadium.
—Roberto Clemente.

The series returned to Baltimore to determine the 1971 champion, and Roberto Clemente was just warming up. The Pirates started Bob Moose, who was one-third of the "meat of the pitching staff," which also included Bob Veale and John Lamb. Hall of Famer Jim Palmer returned for his second start of the series, and Clemente wasted no time making his presence felt, taking two balls and lining the third pitch to right-center for a hustling triple with Bob Prince, in his prime, making the national radio call. Although he was stranded at third and did not like the hitting background (or much else) at Memorial Stadium due to a group of white houses beyond center field, Clemente sliced the first offering from Palmer in his next at bat over the right-field wall for the Pirates' second run. His next two at bats against Palmer involved four pitches and resulted in two hard-hit, deep fly-ball outs to center field. With the score tied 2–2 in the ninth, Clemente let the cannon attached to his right shoulder do the talking.

Clemente could find the ball in New York and throw out a guy in
Pennsylvania.
—Vin Scully

Some right fielders have rifles for arms, but he has a howitzer.
—Tim McCarver

It was a no-hop rope from the right-field warning track, a signature Clemente turn and throw in one motion, that froze Mark Belanger at third, saving the game in a 2–2 tie in the bottom of the ninth inning in Game 6. Davey

Johnson ended the inning with a groundout to short. Although the Pirates went on to lose the game in ten innings, it did not diminish the timing and importance. A stat to ponder: The most right-field assists in major league history are by Roberto Clemente (261). Hank Aaron is second with 186. It's not even close. Clemente has the field lapped. You can check out the video on YouTube. It is one of the best throws of all time, and it was in the bottom of the ninth inning of a tied Game 6 of the World Series. Awesome.

His last at bat for the day was, not surprisingly, an intentional walk in the tenth.

Cumulative Batting Line
R. Clemente

GP	AB	R	H	2B	3B	HR	RBI	BB	SO	AVG	PA	TB	Pitches
6	25	3	11	2	1	1	3	2	1	.440	27	18	85

Game 7: Sunday, October 17, 1971
Attendance: 47,291
Memorial Stadium

Feel the tension—man what a ride.
—*"Hot Rod Race," by George Wilson and covered by Commander Cody and the Lost Planet Airmen*

Poor Earl Weaver, he's down to his last 20-game winner.
—*Curt Gowdy*

Game 7 was started by Clemente's least-favorite 20-game winner, Mike Cuellar. He was opposed by a red-hot Steve Blass, who was coming off a complete-game 5–1 victory in Game 3. Clemente's first at bat started slowly, taking three pitches before hitting a slow chopper to short. In his second at bat in the fourth, he knocked the first pitch out of the park, over the left-field wall no less. This was one of the few balls he hit to the left side and gave the Pirates a lead they would not relinquish. His third at bat against Cuellar was a first-pitch line-out to center. The Pirates added to their lead and took a 2–1 advantage into the ninth inning, setting the stage for Clemente's last World Series at bat against—you guessed it—another 20-game winner, Pat Dobson. The first three pitches were low balls, as Dobson did not want to give the Great One anything to hit. Clemente was taking all the way for strike one, then fouled a ball off the screen for a 3-2 count. With Clemente protecting the plate, there were two more fouls before he swung and missed at a changeup curve ball. An eight-pitch battle ended with only his second strikeout of the series. The Pirates held off the Orioles in the bottom of the ninth to win. Bruce Kison and his best man, Bob Moose, boarded a waiting helicopter to be whisked off to Kison's wedding.

Final Batting Line
R. Clemente

GP	AB	R	H	2B	3B	HR	RBI	BB	SO	AVG	PA	TB	Pitches
7	29	4	12	2	1	2	4	2	2	.414	31	22	98

Clemente's statement was made, and he finally received the national recognition he craved and richly deserved. He was named the first Spanish-speaking World Series Most Valuable Player. Teammate Manny Sanguillén called him the "Bambino Latino." Even though Game 7 in Baltimore was not a sellout, it did not dim his accomplishment. Over nine fateful days in October, seven games, 29 official at bats (not including 2 walks), he batted .414, with 12 hits, including 2 home runs, 2 doubles and 1 triple and only 2 strikeouts. Even though 78 percent of his balls were hit to center or right, he pulled a home run to left in Game 7. He used his legs to beat out base hits and extend a double to a triple. He used his intimidating arm and fielding prowess to hold runners. He even tried, unsuccessfully, to call a time-out when a teammate "missed" a bunt sign. Robert Clemente was a total team player who played with a chip on his shoulder and an insatiable will to win.

7

SEPTEMBER 1, 1971

THE HEROES OF THIS GREAT DAY IN THE INTEGRATION OF MAJOR LEAGUE BASEBALL

By David Finoli

For most of the great events of integration in sports, it is easy to determine the exact moment they took place. On April 15, 1947, Jackie Robinson broke the color barrier in modern baseball history by playing his first game for the Brooklyn Dodgers. On April 8, 1975, Frank Robinson was recognized as the first African American manager (although we find out later in this book that may not be the case). On September 1, 1971, nobody knew that an important moment in major league history was about to occur. Hell, most of the players didn't even realize it for a couple of innings. The Pittsburgh papers were on strike, and without social media, the city was in the dark about such a historic occurrence. Few noticed that the Pittsburgh Pirates had become the first major league team to field a lineup comprised exclusively of players of color. This chapter celebrates the important figures on this momentous occasion.

The headlines around the country for the Associated Press story were as follows: "Bucs Scorch Phillies," "Bucs Club Phillies," "Pirates Outslug Phillies, 10–7." There was no mention of the importance of the day in the article. In fact, the hero of the contest who was mentioned was Luke Walker, who shut down the Philadelphia offense over the final six innings, limiting it to 1 run on 2 hits. The closest mention of the game's significance was Bill Conlin's article on the contest in the September 2, 1971 *Philadelphia Daily News*: "Murtaugh said of his all-soul lineup." But Conlin didn't elaborate

Pitching to the left is Pirate fireballer Bob Veale. Arguably the greatest strikeout pitcher in team history, Veale, as of 2022, owns four of the team's top ten single-season strikeout marks, including 276 in 1965, which is the highest amount in the twentieth century. *Courtesy of the Pittsburgh Pirates.*

on what he was talking about, most likely not realizing that this was a historic lineup.

While many ignored the importance of the day, United Press International did realize the significance and printed it in the papers that carried its account of the day. In the *Kenosha (WI) News,* the article stated that this was believed to be the first time in the history of the game that an all-Black lineup was put on the field. When asked about it, Murtaugh said: "When it comes to making out the lineup, I'm colorblind, and my athletes know it. They don't know it because I told them, but they know it because they're familiar with the way I operate."

Gene Clines questioned Dave Cash about whether this was the first time, "We've started nine brothers before, haven't we?" Before Cash had time to answer, Willie Stargell chimed in that they had started eight in 1967 but that pitcher Dennis Ribant was white.

Despite the lack of accreditation at the time, it was the first time this had happened. Walker was considered the star in most articles of the day. What follows are the names of the true stars of this moment and how they played that day.

Batting First, Second Baseman Rennie Stennett

Stennett became known as the first and only modern-day major league player to collect seven hits in a nine-inning game. But in 1971, he was a twenty-two-year-old rookie who would hit .353 that season. While I was disappointed that Danny Murtaugh put José Pagán on the postseason roster that year instead of Stennett, with José's series-winning double in Game 7, it turned out to be the correct decision. In 1977, while hitting .336, Stennett suffered a severe fracture to his right leg and dislocated his ankle sliding into second. It curtailed his career; he was never the same again. Al Oliver told a reporter for the *New York Times* that he felt that, had Rennie not been injured, he would have had a Hall of Fame career.

Unfortunately, Rennie passed away in May 2021 after a battle with cancer.

In the historic game, Stennett had a first-inning infield single before coming home on Roberto Clemente's single to center. In the third inning, the second baseman singled again, to center off Bucky Brandon, knocking in Jackie Hernández.

BATTING SECOND, CENTER FIELDER GENE CLINES

With the left-handed Woody Fryman on the mound, Gene Clines got the call in center. He was a twenty-four-year-old star in 1971. After hitting .405 in 37 at bats in 1970, he hit .308 in 1971 with 15 stolen bases. He was told by a batboy on this evening that it looked like the Homestead Grays, the famed Negro league team, was on the field. Clines looked out and realized what the batboy meant.

Following his playing career, Clines became a major league and minor league coach. He sadly passed away in January 2022.

Clines had 2 hits and 2 runs in this contest, singling to center in the second and then coming home on a Willie Stargell lineout to right. He doubled to right in the sixth before being knocked in by a Clemente single to make the score 9–7, Pittsburgh.

BATTING THIRD, RIGHT FIELDER ROBERTO CLEMENTE

There is no more beloved player in Pittsburgh sports history than Roberto Clemente. He is the lone player to accumulate 3,000 hits in a Pirates uniform, and in two World Series he had a hit in each of the 14 games he participated in. The 1971 season was special for this iconic figure. He took the team on his back and, at the age of thirty-seven, showed just what a magnificent talent he was, leading the team to their memorable upset of the Baltimore Orioles. A little over a year later, he was gone, killed in a plane crash while trying to take supplies to earthquake-ravaged Nicaragua. The five-year eligibility was waived as he was elected to the Baseball Hall of Fame immediately.

On this historic day, he raised his batting average to .341, knocking in Rennie Stennett with a single to center in the first, walking in the second and getting his second RBI of the day with a single to left in the bottom of the sixth to score Clines.

BATTING FOURTH, LEFT FIELDER WILLIE STARGELL

While Clemente was the leader of this team, "Pops," as Willie Stargell was later known, would lead his own Pirate team eight years later to a world championship. That year, he won the NLCS, World Series and regular-season MVP awards.

Finishing with 475 homers, a figure that would have certainly eclipsed the 500 plateau if not for having to play in cavernous Forbes Field the first part of his career, Stargell was elected to the Baseball Hall of Fame in 1988. He died the morning that PNC Park was about to open in 2001. He failed to recover from an operation to remove his gallbladder.

Stargell doubled home Clemente in a shot to the gap in right in the second inning to tie the game, 2–2. He then hit a sacrifice to right in the second, scoring Clines to once again tie things up, 6–6. He then singled in the fourth.

BATTING FIFTH, CATCHER MANNY SANGUILLÉN

Even though Johnny Bench would eventually surpass Manny Sanguillen in his baseball career, there was only one catcher in the early 1970s who could be mentioned along with the Reds future Hall of Fame catcher, and that was Sangy.

He was a free-swinging hitter who had unusual speed for a catcher. Finishing over .300 for the third consecutive season in 1971 with a .319 average, Manny brought his average up to .331 on September 1 with a 2-for-4 performance that included a single to left in the first and his sixth home run of the season in the second, which scored Clemente to put Pittsburgh up for good, 8–6.

Today, Pirate fans can see their hero at PNC Park, as he has a barbecue stand at the stadium named after him.

BATTING SIXTH, THIRD BASEMAN DAVE CASH

Normally the team's second baseman, Dave Cash was shifted over to third in place of Richie Hebner for this contest. In 1971, the twenty-three-year-old was considered an up-and-coming star. He hit .289 for the season and in 1974 was dealt to the Phillies, where he reached his potential, including a phenomenal 1975 campaign in which he led the National League in hits with 213 while hitting .305. He finished a career-high thirteenth in the MVP voting that season.

Cash was proud to be part of history, but in an article in the *Tribune Review* on August 30, 2021, to celebrate the fiftieth anniversary of the contest, he exclaimed, "We were concentrating more on winning the ballgame than the color of the skin of the guys who were going to be playing."

Following his playing days, Cash worked in investments before becoming a minor league coach and manager.

For the game, he had a single in the first that plated Stargell and gave the Pirates a 3–2 lead. He walked in the seventh.

BATTING SEVENTH, FIRST BASEMAN AL OLIVER

This was the move by Murtaugh that allowed the first all-Black lineup to become a reality. Normally, he would have started Bobby Robertson at first against left-handers, which Woody Fryman, the Philadelphia starter was. Surprisingly, Murtaugh chose to start the left-handed Al Oliver.

Oliver, who hit .303 for his career with 2,743 hits, should garner more serious consideration for the Baseball Hall of Fame than he does. He was also proud to be part of this historic event and is frustrated it doesn't get more recognition. In the same *Trib* article mentioned above, Al said, "Of course Jackie Robinson was definitely history. The all-minority should be maybe second or third [in important baseball integration history], but it has been overlooked and kind of overshadowed, no doubt about that."

Today, Oliver is a licensed minister and motivational speaker.

He had a great game on this afternoon, with a first-inning double that plated Sangy and a leadoff third-inning single to right.

BATTING EIGHTH, SHORTSTOP JACKIE HERNANDEZ

Coming to the Pirates before the 1971 season from Kansas City as a replacement for the oft-injured Gene Alley, Jackie Hernandez had a fan on the club who seemed to be his biggest supporter, Roberto Clemente, who was impressed with what he had seen from Hernandez in Puerto Rico years before. He was known primarily for his defense and is remembered for his phenomenal play to end Game 7 of the 1971 World Series and give the Bucs the world championship.

Sadly, he died in October 2019.

Hernandez was the only hitter for the team not to get a hit in the game. He did knock in Cash in the first inning with a sacrifice fly and walked in the fifth but went 0-for-2 in the contest.

BATTING NINTH, PITCHER DOCK ELLIS

Dock Ellis was known more for his off-the-field antics, such as wearing curlers onto the field before one contest and reportedly pitching a no-hitter against the Padres in 1970 while on LSD, but make no mistake: in 1971, he was one of the best pitchers in the game. He was 19-9 with a 3.06 ERA and made history when he and Vida Blue started the All-Star Game, marking the first time African Americans were the starting pitchers in the midsummer classic.

Ellis had issues with drugs through his career but eventually became sober and dedicated his life to helping others overcome their addictions. He passed away in 2008 from cirrhosis of the liver.

While among the best in the game during this season, on this day, Ellis was anything but great, giving up 5 runs on 4 walks and 2 hits during his inning and a third on the mound.

Number 17, Dock Ellis, is mobbed by his teammates after tossing a no-hitter against the San Diego Padres on June 12, 1970. Dock, who claimed he pitched the gem under the influence of LSD, was unusually wild that night, walking 8 on his way to the 2–0 victory. *Courtesy of the Pittsburgh Pirates.*

RELIEF PITCHER BOB VEALE

After Murtaugh pulled Ellis, he inserted Bob Moose into the game, ending the all-Black lineup. He then pulled Moose in the third and put in Bob Veale, once again giving the Bucs a historic lineup. Veale had been one of the premier strikeout pitchers in the 1960 and still holds many records for the franchise.

Even though he was near the end of his career in 1971 and confined to the bullpen, mostly in mop-up roles, he struck out the only batter he faced, Ron Stone, with men on first and second to end the inning.

8

GENE BAKER

HIS UNKNOWN AND UNCELEBRATED PLACE IN MAJOR LEAGUE HISTORY

By David Finoli

O n April 8, 1975, Frank Robinson managed his first game for the Cleveland Indians. It was a special day at Cleveland Stadium, as the Hall of Famer hit a first-inning home run off Yankee hurler Doc Medich (a player-manager that season). The Indians won that day, giving Robinson his first major league victory. It was an important day as well because Robinson was the first African American to be hired as a full-time manager at the major league level, twenty-eight years after Jackie Robinson made his debut as the first Black player in the modern era of the game.

It was a celebratory day for sure. Not to minimize its importance, but Robinson was not the first African American to manage an MLB contest. Many thought that Ernie Banks had been the first when he took over for Whitey Lockman on May 8, 1973, after Lockman was ejected from the game. Years later, it was proven that Banks wasn't the first. *Pittsburgh Post-Gazette* reporter Elizabeth Bloom documented that another man had managed a game ten years earlier. That honor went to a coach for the Pittsburgh Pirates, Gene Baker, who took over as manager on September 21, 1963, when Danny Murtaugh was tossed out of a contest for arguing with an umpire. He turned to Baker on his way to the locker room to let him know he was now in charge. And history was made.

It's a history that for the most part is forgotten and claimed by some to be nonexistent, as it was only two innings of one game. While Baker's stint as

Danny Murtaugh (*left*) and catcher Hal Smith celebrate after the Pirates won the 1960 World Series. Murtaugh would not only go on to be one of the greatest managers in franchise history, but he also set the first lineup of all players of color in major league history, on September 1, 1971. *Courtesy of the Pittsburgh Pirates.*

manager won't necessarily pass Robinson in importance to integration of the game, it nonetheless is an achievement and worthy of proper recognition. For Baker, it wasn't his only time breaking a barrier in sports. In fact, he had done it on a couple of occasions, making this mostly forgotten player an important figure in the integration of the game.

Baker and a lesser-known player at the time by the name of Ernie Banks, who had been playing shortstop with the Kansas City Monarchs, were promoted to the Chicago Cubs in mid-September 1953. They were the first two African Americans to be on the Cubs roster. Baker had been with the organization since 1950. He played well with the Los Angeles Angels of the Pacific Coast League, and many wondered when he'd finally get his shot. In 1953, he was twenty-eight years old, and with shortstop Roy Smalley Jr. floundering in the field, it was expected that Baker would take over immediately and become the Cubs' first Black player. Unfortunately, Baker was injured when he came up and would not debut for six days. The honor of the first African American to play in a Cub uniform went to Banks, who by the end of the season had solidified his spot as the franchise's shortstop. In 1954, Baker was moved to second and had a fine campaign, combining with Banks to become the first Black double-play combo in major league history.

In 1957, at thirty-two years old, he was dealt to the Bucs with Dee Fondy for Dale Long and Lee Walls. He became the team's utility infielder, starting most of his games at third base while hitting .266 for the club. He was released a year later then was signed once again by the club in 1960. Even though he didn't play much (just 40 plate appearances for Pittsburgh), he nonetheless was a part of their championship season.

General Manager Joe L. Brown liked the thirty-six-year-old infielder despite having cut him from the roster in 1961. He quickly named Baker manager of the Bucs' Class D minor league affiliate in Batavia, New York, in the New York–Pennsylvania League and thus Baker became the first Black manager in organized baseball. He became organized baseball's first African American coach a year later, when he was promoted to the Columbus Jets as a player-coach.

That same season, Hall of Famer Buck O'Neill was hired as a coach for the San Francisco Giants, costing Baker a third shot at becoming a pioneer.

In 1963, the Pirates brought him up to the majors to be part of Murtaugh's staff, making him the second Black coach in major league history, behind O'Neill. It was during this season that the infielder found his way into perhaps his most important moment in the integration of the game.

On September 21, the Pirates were coming to the end of a disappointing season, standing at 72-82. They were facing the Dodgers, who eventually captured the National League pennant, at Dodger Stadium. Pittsburgh was up, 3–2, in the bottom of the eighth and had just gotten Sandy Koufax out of the contest. He was replaced by Ron Perranoski. With 2 outs and the bases full, Bill Virdon hit a ball back to the pitcher and was called out on a close play at first. Both Murtaugh and first-base coach Frank Oceak were incensed at what they deemed a poor call. They argued vehemently and were tossed out of the game. Murtaugh told Baker he was in charge as he went into the dugout. In a May 21, 2018 article by Josh Timmers on bleedcubbieblue.com, Vern Law was quoted as saying that Baker looked at him surprisingly and asked, "Are you sure?" Murtaugh told him he was, and Baker became the first Black manager at the major league level.

Unfortunately, Bucs reliever Tommy Sisk gave up a 3-run walk-off homer to Los Angeles' Willie Davis to end the contest, a 5–3 Dodger victory. But the main memory from this contest was the fact that Gene Baker became a pioneer in the fight for racial equality for the third time in his career. The moment is still mostly forgotten, but it shouldn't be.

II
BASKETBALL

9

ONE OF A KIND

CUM POSEY STANDS ALONE IN SPORTS HISTORY

By Robert Healy III

Whean North American sports fans talk about great multisport figures of the twentieth and twenty-first centuries, some names come to mind right away: Bo Jackson, Deion Sanders, Michael Jordan and Dave Winfield. Other names require more thought but still end up on most lists: Jim Thorpe, Jim Brown, John Elway and even Brian Jordan, Charlie Ward and Babe Didrikson Zaharias. Maybe even Danny Ainge, Tom Glavine and Tim Tebow.

Canadians won't let you forget about Lionel Conacher, and for good reason. Conacher was a Stanley Cup and Grey Cup champion and is a member of the Canadian Football Hall of Fame, Canadian Lacrosse Hall of Fame and Hockey Hall of Fame.

If Conacher's name sounds familiar to Pittsburghers, it's because the "Big Train" was an early twentieth-century standout for the Pittsburgh Yellow Jackets of the United States Amateur Hockey Association and the Pittsburgh Pirates of the NHL. He also played football for local Duquesne University about that same time, becoming one of Pittsburgh's earliest heavily celebrated multisport stars.

Pittsburghers are quick to call out Dick Groat, too, as belonging to the continent's legendary list of jocks. Groat, hailing from Swissvale, Pennsylvania, played fourteen seasons of professional baseball, all in the majors and all but one coming after a promising rookie season in the NBA, where he was a first-round draft pick.

Cumberland Posey (*third from left, middle row*) with the Homestead Grays. He would go on to a legendary career as the Grays' owner after a magnificent basketball career. Posey, to this date, is the only person elected to both the Baseball and Basketball Halls of Fame. *Courtesy of the Pittsburgh Pirates.*

But before Groat, before Conacher and before major media made Pittsburghers aware of out-of-town superstars like Bo and Deion, Pittsburgh was home to a legendary multisport athlete-turned-entrepreneur named Cum Posey.

Historian Rob Ruck says that famous sportswriter Wendell Smith called Posey the "outstanding athlete of the Negro race [of the 1920s]."

The Black Fives Foundation, an organization that works to research and honor the pre-NBA history of African Americans in basketball, seems to support this claim. "Cumberland Willis Posey, Jr. was the best black basketball player of his time," the Black Fives website says. "Playing from the early 1900s through the mid-1920s, [Posey's] peers considered Posey an 'All-Time Immortal.'"

Like Conacher, Posey found his way to Duquesne, where he is recognized as the university's first recorded Black athlete and was inducted in the school's Sports Hall of Fame as a basketball and baseball player.

The *Pittsburgh Tribune-Review* paraphrased Duquesne's president at the time, Charles Dougherty, for a 2016 article that appeared shortly after Posey's selection to the Naismith Memorial Basketball Hall of Fame. "Although what then was known as 'Duquesne University of the Holy Ghost' was tolerant of black students," the article says, "which was unusual at the time, the light-skinned Posey passed as being white because of the intolerance of the school's opponents, Dougherty said."

Posey was a guard, about five feet, nine inches tall, the *Tribune-Review* reported (the Naismith website has him at five feet, four inches) and led Duquesne in scoring for three straight seasons (1916–18) playing under the name—"because of eligibility issues," the *Trib* says—Charles Cumbert.

Before coming to Duquesne, Posey played at Penn State University and possibly the University of Pittsburgh and formed the Monticello Athletic Association's all-Black basketball team. The team, considered to be 1912's Colored Basketball world champions, later became known as the Loendi Big Five and won four more Colored Basketball titles, from 1920 to 1923.

The Naismith site calls Loendi "one of the most dominate [*sic*] teams of the era" and says that "Posey floated quickly and gracefully around the perimeter where he scored most of his points."

Posey also proved, while leading the Loendi squad, to be an adept club operator, which included, according to the Society for American Baseball Research's (SABR) biography on Posey, "managing, booking, and promoting."

Amazingly, Posey balanced those basketball duties for many years with playing for and later managing and owning the famed Negro baseball team the Homestead (formerly Murdock) Grays. SABR reports that Posey became the Grays' captain by 1916 and was a right-handed batter and thrower whose "quickness made him a natural center fielder." The National Baseball Hall of Fame lists Posey's involvement with the Grays as lasting from 1911 until his death in 1946.

"Stemming from his experience with his basketball club," SABR reports, Posey started booking Grays games by 1918 and became team secretary.

Shortly later, Posey worked a deal to purchase the club and, according to the Baseball Hall website, "built the Grays into a perennially powerful and profitable team, one of the best in the East."

Indeed, the Grays won nine consecutive Negro National League pennants (1937–45) and two Negro World Series (1943 and '44) while drawing large crowds to their home games in Pittsburgh and Washington, D.C.

In a 2016 article for the website The Undefeated, "Splash and Cash: The Legend of Old-School Baller Cumberland Posey," writer Jesse Washington paraphrased Ruck: "Sports in this era helped black America forge an identity beyond white control, Ruck said....This was the genesis of African-American professional sports. Posey was a pioneer in every aspect, in both basketball and baseball."

While Posey is in the Naismith Hall as a player, it is his status as a team executive that earned him a plaque in the Baseball Hall of Fame in 2006.

Posey inspired not only more Black involvement in sports administration. He also, Ruck tells Washington, inspired at least one white athlete-turned-executive. Art Rooney was an amateur boxer, amateur basketball and football player and minor professional baseball player from Pittsburgh's North Side who was eleven years Posey's junior and who became a Pro Football Hall of Famer in the contributor category.

"Posey's exploits as an athlete and businessman caught the attention of Art Rooney, future founder of the Pittsburgh Steelers, who attended Duquesne's prep school," Washington writes.

As Ruck told Washington, "They play the same position, point guard, both leadoff batters and center fielders, both of them are incredibly tough. Art models his game after Posey. He learns how to be a promoter after Posey. That's what Art's real genius was. Art was the best all-around white ballplayer in those years. He's the white clone of Posey, off and on the field."

Hard to top a Rooney in Pittsburgh, but Cum Posey has topped the whole world in at least one category. Posey, the Homestead, Pennsylvania native and Black sports pioneer, is the only person (through 2022) enshrined in the major baseball and basketball halls of fame.

10

AN UPSET FOR THE AGES

THE 1912 COLORED WORLD CHAMPION MONTICELLO ATHLETIC ASSOCIATION

By David Finoli

In the list of champions that have represented western Pennsylvania over the years, one of the lesser-known yet most important was the 1912 Monticello Athletic Association, led by baseball and basketball Hall of Famer Cumberland Posey. Their victory over Howard University, a team considered to be the best Black squad in the country, was one of the great upsets in the history of the game.

This contest didn't lead to the direct integration of the game. But it did showcase some of the best basketball of the era and introduce an innovation that would lead to something we know today as the jump shot. It was something Posey brought into the sport, stunning both audiences and Monticello's opponents.

The best basketball played by African American squads in the early 1910s was by Howard University in Washington, D.C. The program was formed by a man who had led the 12th Street Colored YMCA team to the Black world championship in 1909–10, Edwin Henderson. Most of the YMCA team had been attending Howard, so it was easy for him to pull a high percentage of the defending 1910 champs to his new Howard team, putting together a squad that would be very difficult to beat. They were led by Hudson Oliver and Edward Gray, both of whom would go on to be noted physicians. There was also Henry Nixon, who was also a Walter Camp All-American halfback for the Amherst football team;

Charles Gilmore; and two brothers, Maurice and Arthur Curtis. The group continued to excel and captured the 1910–11 world Black championship. They were so strong that it was a foregone conclusion that they would easily defend that title in 1912.

At the time, Pittsburgh was not considered the hub of basketball for African Americans in this country. There was one team of note, the Monticello Athletic Association. Led by Posey, the squad took on the best white teams that western Pennsylvania had to offer and defeated them all. One of their players, Jim Dorsey, was a janitor at the Phipps Gymnasium on the north side of the city. It was reserved for whites only, but Dorsey had a key to the building, which allowed Monticello a nice facility in which to practice.

Along with Posey and Dorsey, the team consisted of Cumberland's brother Seward, Israel Lee, Walter Clark and Sell Hall. With no other Black teams of note in the area, Posey was looking to convince the best to come to the Steel City and challenge the defending champions to travel to Pittsburgh to play his team.

Howard University accepted the challenge with little fear. The game would be played at the Washington Park Fieldhouse, located in the Hill District of the city, not far from where the Civic Arena was built half a century later. The contest was held in front of what was described in a 2008 article on Blackfives.com as "as large and as fine an audience of local society as it would be possible to assemble."

The visitors considered Monticello a team nowhere near their talent level, but their overconfidence became a factor early in the contest. The game was considered the first contest in Pittsburgh between two Black teams, and Monticello was much faster and much more physical than Howard anticipated.

Gilmore, Howard's best offensive player, was held in check by the aggressive defensive play of Hall, who was relatively new to the game. The visitors were having trouble converting from the foul line, and the home team was remarkably on top at the half, 9–8. In the second half, Monticello introduced the world to the jump shot. Gilmore provided the only offense Howard had, scoring 11 of the team's 19 points.

The *Pittsburgh Courier* proclaimed the Pittsburgh five's defensive excellence: "Dorsey, Clark and S. Posey played brilliantly, breaking up most of Howard's plays." While Seward was effective on the defensive side of the ball, it was his Hall of Fame brother Cumberland who was the game's star.

Scoring a game-high 15 points, Posey and Hall both launched shots from much farther away from the basket than was attempted at the time. It helped turn what was a close, 1-point affair into a 24–19 victory that gave Monticello the "colored world championship" for the 1911–12 campaign.

The Washington Park Fieldhouse would eventually be torn down to make way for the Civic Arena, and Posey moved on to run the Loendi Big Five, a club considered the greatest Black team of the era, winning four Black world championships between 1919 and 1922. But it was this young, inexperienced Monticello squad that began it all with one of the greatest upsets the city would ever see.

11

A SON SEARCHES FOR CHUCK COOPER'S
RIGHTFUL PLACE

By Tom Rooney

C huck, we know it's not a matter of 'if' but 'when' your dad gets in the Hall of Fame," said the principal contact in Springfield, Massachusetts, the home of basketball's enshrined heroes of hoops lore. "He didn't get in this time. It'll happen sooner than later."

But Chuck Cooper III, son of the first African American to be drafted by an NBA team, in 1950 by the Boston Celtics, knew it would be at least another long year of waiting and working the phone lines and email trails before he might get "the call" on behalf of his dad.

That call did come in 2019. Chuck later philosophized, "When you're in, you're in forever and nobody remembers how long you waited." But it was a process that took too long and was too frustrating.

That was sort of the pattern of Chuck's dad's life: one dribble forward, two dribbles back—and too much "traveling" along the way when it came to fairness and rightful credit.

A young African American man would lead a life of *Breaking Barriers*, the title of the biography Chuck III cowrote about his dad with David Finoli. But it was a different kind of "break" that almost ended a career as an exceptional amateur and professional athlete.

When the elder Cooper was a child, he idolized his older brother Cornell, the first great athlete in the family. Cornell held the Pittsburgh City Schools record for the high jump for three decades and was known to wager people that he could "high wire" dangerous railings between structures. Trying to emulate "big brother," young Charles fell while trying to walk along a railing on the front porch of the family home in Pittsburgh. A compound fracture was diagnosed. The bone was sticking out of his arm. Doctors recommended amputating the youngster's appendage, but his mother, wary of how quick decisions seemed to be commonly made involving Black patients in order to "get to the next person in line," refused the solution. She insisted they try to save the arm of "Charley" Cooper, and they were successful.

Cooper took a not-so-scenic route to the Hall of Fame. More rightfully obscene-ic than scenic in the number of twists and turns along the way. After starring at Pittsburgh's legendary athlete factory, Westinghouse High School, where he graduated in 1944, he played a semester at West Virginia State College before being drafted into the navy near the end of World War II. He returned to Pittsburgh in two years to attend Duquesne University, where he started all four years and

Chuck Cooper was one of the most legendary players in NBA history. He was the first African American to step on the NBA floor as a player, which he did in an exhibition game against Baltimore, as well as the first to be drafted into the league, the first to start a regular-season game and the first to be named to an all-NBA rookie team. *Courtesy of Duquesne University Athletics.*

was an All-American. His college hoops career ended in March 1950 with a loss in the semifinals to eventual champion City College of New York (CCNY) in the National Invitation Tournament at New York's Madison Square Garden. A notable college game he did not start was one that did not start at all. Highly ranked Tennessee came to Pittsburgh to play, and Duquesne moved the game to a large high school gym in McKeesport. All 2,500 tickets were presold. Tennessee refused to take the court because the Dukes had a Black player.

That player was Chuck Cooper. Duquesne held a player vote: to play without Cooper or to not play at all. The unanimous vote sent the Volunteers back to Tennessee without a game.

Having graduated and because no NBA team had ever drafted a Black player, Cooper did what skilled players of his color desiring to play were left to do: he signed with the Harlem Globetrotters. The 'Trotters of that era were different from today's more entertainment-driven attraction. They barnstormed the country, playing college All-Star teams. An earlier team even beat the NBA champ Minnesota Lakers in front of twenty thousand fans in Chicago. To make the squad was no simple accomplishment. The "Globbies" carried a roster of just twelve, and a player had to be one of the best dozen African American players in the country of any age. Knowing that no African American had ever been drafted by an NBA team, Cooper was happy to verbally commit to play for the Globetrotters.

For Cooper, Globetrotter owner Abe Sapperstein added a sweetener. A movie was planned on the Globetrotters, and Sapperstein promised Cooper he'd star opposite Dorothy Dandridge, a film superstar and the first Black actress to be nominated for an Academy Award in the Best Actress category.

But on April 25 in that graduating year, a month after agreeing to join Sapperstein's Globetrotters, something happened that had never happened before. Walter Brown, owner of the Boston Celtics of the National Basketball Association, selected Cooper in the second round of the annual draft. An executive from another team shot a surprised glance across the table at Brown and said, "Walter, you can't take him, he's colored." Brown stared the man down and replied, "I don't care if he's striped, plaid or polka dot, Boston takes Charles Cooper of Duquesne." Cooper chose the parquet-floored Boston Garden over the Hollywood lights, and Sapperstein let the recent college graduate out of his verbal agreement.

Cooper played six seasons in the NBA for the Celtics, St. Louis Hawks and Fort Wayne Pistons. Although he did not face the level of racism that Jackie Robinson experienced a few years before when he broke the "color line" in Major League Baseball, there was some of that, especially in restaurants and hotels along the way when the team played in the South for preseason games. And college hoops ruled basketball in those days, even to the point where big matchups would chase the New York Knicks out of Madison Square Garden into smaller venues. Commonly, NBA teams saw their biggest draws on nights when they agreed to be part of a doubleheader: two NBA teams squaring off in a regular-season game, and the Globetrotters playing their own opponent as the closer.

Ever the trailblazer, Cooper pulled off two other important firsts after his playing days. He became the City of Pittsburgh's first Black department head and then, later, what is now PNC Corporation's first Black executive. He was still working at Pittsburgh National Bank (now PNC) when he passed away from cancer at age fifty-seven.

Chuck Cooper III was twenty-one when his father died, and he immediately began to make sure his father's legacy would survive and thrive. It was a challenge that differed from that of other former notable NBA players, for

Chuck Cooper (15) jumping over his opponent for a layup, was one of the greatest players to don a Duquesne basketball uniform. He not only was the second player to join the 1,000-point club in his career on the Bluff, but he also set the single-season scoring mark his junior year. *Courtesy of Duquesne University Athletics.*

a number of reasons. There was no NBA team in Pittsburgh to attach a campaign for Cooper. Chuck Cooper's dad was no longer around to be celebrated and tell his story, having died so young. And there was confusion nationally about another Charles Cooper who was already in the Naismith Hall of Fame as a former player in the sport's one time Negro leagues.

"I can't tell how many times people congratulated me, or were surprised that I was still promoting my dad's candidacy for the Hall," Copper III remembered. "There was an early Basketball Negro leagues player, Charles 'Tarzan' Cooper, who was already enshrined. They thought that was my dad. When I explained and then mentioned that my dad, a different Charles Cooper, wasn't in the Hall, they were shocked."

The younger Cooper's first public testimony to his father was reclaiming the local basketball court near their Pittsburgh home. "Gang members with the monster trucks were parking right on the court, locking the kids out. I got involved, started my own basketball program in my dad's name and even extended that to baseball," Cooper said. "It was sad and rewarding at the same time when the handful of kids I was working with suddenly turned into thirty kids waiting on the sideline…kids who lacked access to facilities, equipment and leadership. They needed positive role models when, really, they were instead being exposed to gangs and no leadership!"

It was through his dad's high school teammate and future Pro Football Hall of Famer Bill Nunn that things started to gel on a broader level. Duquesne University and the Rooney Sports & Entertainment Group of Pittsburgh were developing a new basketball event they wanted to call the "Chuck Cooper Classic." In tracking down the Cooper family, with whom Duquesne had lost touch, Nunn made the connection for them for his boyhood friend. PNC Bank, Chuck Cooper's final employer, stepped up to not only sponsor the new basketball event but also help the younger Cooper fund the start of the Chuck Cooper Foundation, a 501(c)(3) that in its first ten years distributed over $320,000 in scholarships to graduate students of color.

The Cooper Foundation board took it upon itself to work with Chuck to get his father's candidacy for the Hall of Fame seriously considered. Two other Black players who shared the elder Cooper's "first" distinction had already been inducted into the Hall of Fame. In that historic NBA season of 1950, Nathaniel "Sweetwater" Clifton was the first to have a relationship with an NBA team, as his contract with the Globetrotters was sold to the New York Knicks. Earl Lloyd, drafted seven rounds later than Cooper in 1950, was the first to actually play in an NBA game, due to a scheduling nuance, by one day, as his Washington team opened their season on a Friday night and Cooper's Celtics didn't open their season until the following night. Clifton and Lloyd already had their lives and careers celebrated in Springfield. Where was Chuck Cooper's honor?

Chuck III and his support group saw the effort finally pay off in 2019 after five years of pushing every button possible. The induction saw a who's who of basketball greats on the stage as co-presenters when Charles Henry Cooper was posthumously inducted into the hallowed hall in Springfield, Massachusetts, where the game of basketball was invented by a YMCA instructor named Dr. James Naismith in 1891.

The son was overwhelmed when a sterling cast of past inductees came onstage at the ceremony to induct his dad into the Hall of Fame: Bill Russell, Tom Heinsohn, Ray Allen, Dominique Wilkins, Elgin Baylor, Kareem Abdul-Jabbar, Mannie Jackson, Julius Irving, Larry Bird and Isiah Thomas. "My dad wasn't physically there, of course, but *he was there*, I know. And talk about a welcoming committee!" his proud son remembered. "We heard for years it was just a matter of time he'd get in, but the time mattered to us. Hey, we're good now."

DUQUESNE UNIVERSITY OPENS ITS DOORS

By David Finoli

In the late 1940s, the Brooklyn Dodgers opened its doors to Black players, starting in 1947, when Jackie Robinson broke the color barrier in Major League Baseball. It led to a successful era in the National League that saw them win six of ten pennants between 1947 and 1956, including their first World Series title. Branch Rickey was unafraid to sign some of the best players the Negro leagues had to offer, while other franchises struggled to overcome their prejudice against Black athletes and were apprehensive to integrate. In college basketball, many programs, especially in the South, also had issues integrating. Duquesne University was one that not only opened its doors to Black athletes but also did so in an aggressive manner in the 1950s. Like the Dodgers, the Dukes enjoyed the finest era in their program's history when they weren't afraid to take the best players regardless of the color of their skin.

While the majority of this historic story took place between 1946 and 1956 with integration on the Bluff (the nickname of the location of Duquesne University), in 1916, the school integrated for the first time when Cumberland Posey took the court for the school. The following are biographies of the great African Americans who came to Duquesne during this period.

CUMBERLAND POSEY

Posey played for the Dukes for three seasons between 1916 and 1918 and led them in scoring each season. At Duquesne, he played under the name Charles W. Cumbert so that he could preserve his amateur standing and play for Duquesne University of the Holy Ghost, as it was called at the time. While there, he was also captain of the golf team.

Following his college career, Posey went on to lead the Loendi Big Five to four consecutive Black basketball world championships. He eventually left basketball and concentrated on the position he became noted for in sports history: the legendary owner of the Homestead Grays. He turned the team into arguably the most successful Negro league baseball franchise in the history of the league.

In 2006, he was given the ultimate honor when he was elected to the Baseball Hall of Fame. Ten years later, he made history, becoming not only the first Duquesne player to be named to the Naismith Basketball Hall of Fame but also the only athlete to be elected to both the baseball and basketball Halls of Fame.

CHUCK COOPER

After playing his freshman season at West Virginia State and then a stint in the navy during the final stages of World War II, Chuck Cooper decided to come home to continue his collegiate basketball career. Legendary Dukes coach Charles "Chick" Davies recruited Cooper to the Bluff, where he was given four full seasons to play despite his previous college experience.

Perhaps the most notable date in Cooper's historic career came during his freshman season, when Duquesne took on Tennessee at McKeesport High School. It was here where the school showed it was serious about integrating the sport. Volunteer coach John Maurer told Davies that his team would refuse to take the court unless Davies guaranteed that he would not play Cooper. Cooper offered to sit out so that the game could go on, but the team didn't want to play unless Chuck played. Most important, Judge Sammy Weiss, who was the acting chairman of the school's athletic committee, wouldn't send the team on the court unless Maurer backed off. The Tennessee coach refused, and Weiss walked on to the court and announced that the game would be canceled and sent the Volunteers home.

Chuck Cooper, shown above, had been forgotten by many long after his career ended. Thanks to his son, Chuck Cooper III, his memories and accomplishments were brought to the forefront again. His son set up a foundation in his name, and his efforts for his father to be remembered eventually led to his rightful induction into the Naismith Basketball Hall of Fame. *Courtesy of Duquesne University Athletics.*

The support meant so much to Cooper, who became a First-Team All-American his senior season, set the single-season scoring mark his junior year and became the second player in school history to garner 1,000 points in his career. Most important, he made history as the first African American selected in the NBA draft when he was taken in the second round by the Boston Celtics. In 2019, he became the second Duquesne player elected to the Naismith Basketball Hall of Fame.

JIM TUCKER

Integration in the North for college basketball was rare in the early 1950s; integration in the South was nonexistent. A star player for Paris (Kentucky)

Western High School, Jim Tucker so impressed the legendary Kentucky coach Adolph Rupp that he visited Tucker in the locker room. While Rupp told the high school star that he wouldn't be able to recruit a Black player at the time to Kentucky, he thought he had All-American potential and would call some northern coaches he thought might be interested in Tucker. The coach he called was Dudey Moore, who felt that if a coach as great as Rupp was impressed, then Jim Tucker was good enough for him.

Both Rupp and Moore were correct, as Tucker became a Second-Team All-American his sophomore year in 1952 while leading the Dukes to a 70-15 mark in four seasons, including a number four ranking in 1952 and a trip to the National Invitation Tournament (NIT) finals his senior year.

While at Duquesne, he became the first player to eclipse 500 points in a season, scoring 512 in 1952. He was just the third player to break the 1,000-point barrier.

It was in the NBA that he made history, not only becoming the first African American, with Earl Lloyd, to be part of a championship team, capturing the title in 1955 with Syracuse, but he also had the fastest triple double in the league's history, achieving it on February 20, 1955, against the Knicks. The mark held for sixty-three years, until Nikola Jokić of the Nuggets broke it on February 15, 2018.

FLETCHER JOHNSON

Fletcher Johnson may be the least known of the Dukes' African American players of the 1950s. But make no mistake: he was extremely talented.

According to his obituary in the *New York Post* on October 14, 2008, when Fletcher was in high school, he contacted Haskell Cohen, who eventually became the publicity director for the NBA but at the time was a writer for the *Pittsburgh Courier*. He told Cohen that he wanted to play for Dudey Moore and the Dukes and wanted to know if Cohen could mention that to Moore. When asked why he should do that, Johnson responded that he could outjump the great Sherman White from Long Island University. When Cohen contacted White and found out it was true, Fletcher soon became a member of the Dukes.

He was an important sixth man for Moore and averaged 12.6 points per game his junior season in 1953. Johnson was drafted in the ninth round of the NBA draft in 1954 by the Syracuse Nationals but ended up playing in Europe, where he earned his medical degree from the University of Geneva.

While not a Hall of Fame basketball player, Fletcher became one of the country's preeminent cardiovascular surgeons, working out of three hospitals in New York City until he passed away from pancreatic cancer in 2008.

DICK RICKETTS

Dick Ricketts is in the conversation for greatest player in the history of Duquesne basketball. Coming out of Pottstown High School, Ricketts was offered a pro baseball contract before turning it down to play both baseball and basketball on the Bluff.

It proved to be a fortuitous decision for both the player and the team, as Ricketts not only hit over .400 in his baseball career at Duquesne but also set marks for points in a career (1,963) and rebounds (1,359), both records that still stand today. His number 12 hangs from the rafters at the UPMC Cooper Fieldhouse, never to be worn again.

The Dukes were rated in the top ten for each of his four seasons at the school, and in 1955, he was the driving force, along with Sihugo Green, in leading the school to its lone national championship with a victory in the 1955 NIT.

Dick Ricketts (12) is arguably the greatest player to don a Duquesne uniform. He was a consensus First-Team All-American in 1955 while leading the Dukes to their lone national championship in the NIT. After being selected first overall by the St. Louis Hawks in the 1955 NBA draft, he went on to a career in baseball, debuting with the St. Louis Cardinals on June 14, 1959. *Courtesy of Duquesne University Athletics.*

Ricketts was a three-time All-American, selected Second-Team his sophomore year, a consensus Second-Team a year later and finishing up his career on the Bluff being named a First-Team consensus All-American his senior year.

He went on to be the first player chosen in the 1955 NBA draft and had a short career with Cincinnati before exclusively playing baseball, where he made the majors with the St. Louis Cardinals in 1955.

Sihugo Green

In an era when basketball was played by passing station-to-station and looking for an open shot, Sihugo Green (shown cutting to the basket for a layup) played a more modern version of the game with his exceptional athletic talent. He is the only two-time consensus First-Team All-American in Duquesne history. *Courtesy of Duquesne University Athletics.*

While basketball was played in a station-to-station manner in the 1950s, Sihugo Green's athletic skills put him on a level that wasn't seen during the time and wouldn't be seen for at least twenty more years. It helped him become arguably the greatest talent ever seen in the history of basketball at Duquesne.

Finishing his career with 1,605 points in three seasons, Green was also a great rebounder, garnering 11.5 per game despite the fact that he was only six feet, two inches tall. He and Dick Ricketts made for an unstoppable force in 1954 and 1955, helping lead the team to its only national championship in 1955. Green and Ricketts accounted for all 35 points the team scored in the first half of their 70–58 victory over Dayton in the NIT finals.

Coming out of Boys High School in Brooklyn, where he was a member of the All-Metropolitan New York team and averaged 25 points per game, Green was described as quirky. He felt he couldn't jump unless he had his jumping socks on and often complained about one malady or another.

Throughout it all, he was an incredible player. The only Duquesne player ever to be named consensus First-Team All-American twice (1955 and 1956), he was the first player drafted in the 1956 NBA draft. He and Dick Ricketts became the first players from the same school to be drafted number one overall in the history of the league. It's a distinction they still hold today.

Green has the honor of having his number 11 hanging from the rafters at the UPMC Cooper Fieldhouse.

Dave Ricketts

Make no mistake, Dave Ricketts was nowhere near the basketball talent his brother Dick was, but he was an important starter on the 1955 NIT champion Duquesne Dukes in his sophomore season and went on to have a solid career on the Bluff. He led the team in scoring his senior season, averaging 17.9 points per game in 1957. That year, he eclipsed his brother's national record of 39 consecutive free throws made, hitting on 42 straight from the free-throw line. For his efforts, Dave was given the Samuel Weiss Award, presented to the top student athlete at Duquesne.

After following his brother to Duquesne in basketball, Dave chose baseball, signing with the St. Louis Cardinals following a short time in the army. While he wasn't the equal to Dick on the basketball court, he had a better Major League Baseball career as a catcher with the Cards and Pirates.

Duquesne integrated before most college basketball teams in the 1940s and '50s. This was not only important to the success the program had during the period, but it was also something that inspired many who came to the Bluff in the years since. Legendary guard B.B. Flenory requested wearing Chuck Cooper's number 11 after signing with the Boston Celtics following his career with the Dukes. He proudly felt that "Duquesne was on the forefront of integration in sports in Pittsburgh. They took a stance with Chuck Cooper when it wasn't a popular thing to do. Society is catching up today with what Duquesne did over sixty years ago. That's the biggest reason I went to Duquesne."

Current women's coach Dan Burt felt that "from Cumberland Posey to Chuck Cooper to former women's coach Dan Durkin, who began recruiting players from overseas before it became popular, Duquesne has always opened its doors to everyone."

It's something that was done nine decades earlier but is still a point of pride in the Duquesne community today.

13

TWO YEARS, TWO MVPs

CONNIE HAWKINS MAKES AN IMPRESSION ON THE CITY OF PITTSBURGH

By David Finoli

I t's easy to see just what an impression Connie Hawkins made on the city of Pittsburgh. He played his first two seasons of professional basketball in the Steel City and won two Most Valuable Player Awards. He also inspired a summer basketball league in the city that is named after him. In 1980, that league was ranked the fifth-best summer league in the country by *Sports Illustrated*. Hawkins's story is an impressive one, especially his second campaign, when he led the Pittsburgh Pipers to the first American Basketball Association championship in 1968. Looking closer, was it the man who brought excellence in professional basketball to the city, or was it the city that saved his Hall of Fame career?

Hawkins was one of the nation's most sought-after high school recruits in 1960, out of Boys High School in New York City, the same school that produced Duquesne great Sihugo Green. He received offers from 125 schools around the country before committing to the University of Colorado. He decided very early in his collegiate career that Boulder was not for him and quickly transferred to the University of Iowa, where he became a star of the Hawkeye freshman team. Unfortunately, it was discovered that he was friends with and received a $200 loan from a man named Jack Molinas, who was accused of a massive college basketball point-shaving scandal that led to the arrest of thirty-seven players. Despite the fact that Hawkins's brother paid the loan back and Connie played freshman ball during the 1960–61 campaign, when the allegations were made, and even though he was never arrested or indicted, he was kicked out of Iowa and effectively blackballed from the NCAA, just because he knew Molinas. His promising basketball career was now very much in limbo. Enter Lenny Litman.

Litman turned down a franchise in the NBA after Pittsburgh Hornets owner John Harris gave up the one he was given because he felt a franchise in the new American Basketball League could compete more quickly than an expansion NBA franchise. Even though Litman's logic eventually turned out to be shortsighted, his eye for talent wasn't. Without a college to call home, Hawkins attended a workout for the city's ABL franchise, the Rens. So impressed was Litman that he offered the nineteen-year-old a contract after league officials cleared him from both his issues with Molinas and the fact his class wouldn't graduate until 1964. (In November, some of the ABL owners still claimed he wasn't eligible to play professional ball because his class hadn't graduated.) Litman said in a United Press International article in many newspapers on November 13, 1961, that, "When we went after Connie it was definitely established by Hawkins and by Iowa that he would not return to the school. Therefore he was no longer a student." Litman was correct; the league agreed, and Connie joined the Rens

He was a superstar in his first professional season despite his young age. Hawkins led the league in scoring during the 1961–62 season, averaging 27.5 points per game, and was awarded the league's first MVP award. The ABL began a second campaign the following year but lasted little less than half a season when it was no longer financially viable. Hawkins played in only 16 of the Rens' 22 games, finishing behind Kansas City's Bill Bridges with a 27.9 per game average in the shortened season.

While he had established himself as a star, he now had nowhere to display his talents. Hawkins signed with the Harlem Globetrotters and then found himself undrafted in the NBA when his class became eligible in 1964. In 1966, the NBA formally banned him, prompting Hawkins to file a lawsuit against the league.

Luckily for the young superstar, another circuit came into existence in 1967, the American Basketball Association, affording Connie another opportunity to play in a professional league as, once again, the city of Pittsburgh came to his rescue.

Gabe Rubin, the owner of the Pittsburgh Pipers, wanted to make a big splash with his new franchise, so he signed an established NBA player, the Detroit Piston center Joe Strawder. He also inked the star Rens player, Hawkins, who exclaimed in a *Pittsburgh Post-Gazette* article on April 29, 1967, that "yes, I'm mighty happy to be back in nationally organized basketball."

Despite having the highly talented Hawkins, the team was stagnant, standing at 11-12 when they swung a deal for forward Art Heyman. The two quickly jelled, and the Pipers ended the campaign 54-24, capturing the Eastern Division crown. Finishing the season as the ABA scoring champion with 26.8 points per game, Hawkins took his skills to another level in the postseason, leading the Pipers through the first two rounds of the playoffs with easy wins over the Indiana Pacers and Minnesota Muskies. They met the New Orleans Buccaneers in the finals. The teams battled back and forth in a classic series. New Orleans took a three-games-to-two lead. Hawkins injured his knee in the fourth game and sat out the fifth.

He had a torn medial tendon, but instead of sitting out Game 6 with the injury, he wrapped his knee and played a game for the ages, scoring 41 points in a 118–112 win and forcing a Game 7 at the Civic Arena in Pittsburgh. A near-sellout crowd of 11,457 fans showed up to see the injured Hawkins net 20 in a 122–113 victory that gave the Pipers the initial ABA championship. Unfortunately for the city, the team was moved to Minneapolis the next year as the Muskies folded and the ABA wanted a team in the city where the league offices were.

He played a little over half a season in Minnesota, where he averaged 30.2 points per game. The NBA lifted its ban on Connie Hawkins, agreeing to a $1.3 million settlement in the lawsuit. Hawkins went on to a Hall of Fame career with Phoenix, the Lakers and Atlanta. Even though the Connie Hawkins story had a chance for a nice finish in the NBA, it was his two years in the Steel City that not only began but perhaps also saved his career.

14

FROM CLAIRTON TO MURRAY STATE

STEW JOHNSON'S HISTORIC JOURNEY

By David Finoli

When Stewart Johnson came out of Clairton High School and went to Murray State, he didn't realize that the path he was about to embark on would make him an important pioneer in the push to integrate sports in this country. Heck, he didn't realize the importance of his journey until he was a sophomore at the school. It was a very difficult path he chose, as it was for all pioneers in the push to make life equitable in the United States for all persons, no matter their color. The path began not far from Pittsburgh, during a happy time for the future American Basketball Association star. Johnson became the first Black player to receive a basketball scholarship at a school that was not a historically Black college and university (HCBU) in the South.

Born in New York City, Johnson and his parents came to Clairton after spending time in New York and also in the South. Most African American children faced a difficult upbringing in the South, and Johnson's parents did not want their children growing up in that atmosphere.

Clairton was known mostly for its football. Johnson recalled:

> *Clairton and the Mon-Valley area have been known for their high school football powers. When I was growing up, basketball was a secondary sport. Everyone played high school football, and if you didn't get injured, you played basketball. We had some great athletes there, and I came around at the right time, because we had some great teammates there, and all*

these guys were multi-sports athletes. Before I graduated, we won the first sectional title ever for our high school. I was having fun. I was sorry to leave high school.

Stewart was impressive, and by the time he left Clairton, he had two hundred collegiate offers. He was considering NYU and Wichita State. He was contacted to go for a visit to Kentucky, who saw his picture in a magazine and didn't realize that he was a Black player. It was the only school he was rejected from. Back in the 1960s, all the pictures of basketball players were in black and white, and if you had a light complexion, schools didn't know if you were a Black player or a white player. "They wanted to recruit me and I was going to be a Kentucky product but I got down there and the assistant coaches told me that Kentucky wasn't ready for a player of color but if I went to a junior college and played a year then perhaps they'd be ready to take on a person of color, so I said 'Thank you, Mr. Rupp [legendary Kentucky coach Adolph Rupp], but no thank you.'"

Johnson wasn't thinking of going to Murray State. "Murray State was never really in the running then. I had never heard of it. I knew nothing about it. I got a letter and a Black gentleman by the name of Pete Rutledge came up, who was my sponsor. He was a city undertaker for Black people, and his job was to talk to my parents and convince them to have me come to the school." Stewart went on to say that "it was a hard sell job, I went down to Murray, Kentucky, and it was Pete and his family that tried to tell me what life in the South was like, because I didn't know. Both my parents were from the South, my mother was from North Carolina and my father was from Virginia. In reality they didn't want me to go down south. Their family's generation before just moved out of the South. They had a cousin that was lynched, and they didn't want me experiencing that kind of life."

Rutledge and legendary Racers coach Cal Luther continued to try to sell Johnson on Murray State. Luther was someone whom Johnson respected. "I had a really good coach by the name of Cal Luther. At the time I did not realize it, but Coach Luther and his family went through nearly as much as I went through. Fans probably screamed at him, 'How could you bring a Black player here', 'We don't want Blacks here'. I think Cal just had the foresight to think that this is the way things are going to be from now on. You want to win, you want the best athletes, and it doesn't matter if they are black, white, green or yellow."

Whatever the reason, Luther had the courage to integrate his school, and it ended up making history, a history that neither Johnson or Luther realized at the time. "I didn't know it at the time, but I wound up being the first NCAA Black student for basketball in the South with a scholarship."

Rutledge and Luther were successful in convincing not only Stewart but also his parents, who were very apprehensive to let their son go to school in the South, to come to Murray, Kentucky, to continue his career. "The most resistance came from my parents, both who were born and raised in the South. This was the time of civil rights, they were blowing up churches and lynching people. The last thing my parents wanted me to do is go to an all-white school in the South in a little town called Murray, Kentucky." The Clairton star recalled his visit and what he saw at Murray. "It was not like it is today. Murray was a typical southern town back then with railroad tracks running through the middle of town. Whites on one side of the tracks and Blacks on the other. If you got caught on the wrong side at the wrong time there could be trouble." Luckily for Johnson, he ended up marrying a local girl, which kept him out of trouble. "My social life was intact, I had her family there and it was good."

Things weren't as tranquil on the court as he began his career at Murray. He got into fights on a daily basis with his teammates. "Most of those players who were there ahead of me had never played against a Black player. Everything was segregated there. I come there with my Clairton/ Pittsburgh swagger, and back home someone calls you a name and you fight. That was happening at basketball practice, but we overcame that."

The same thing was happening during games, especially from his home fans, who were particularly rough on him. "On our home court in the first couple games when they announced my name people would have the audacity to do things like throw black cats at midcourt when they announced my name and I thought, 'Damn, I'm playing for Murray and they're doing this?'" He also had issues in the classroom.

> I had a lot of old professors who had never taught Black students before. There were some who thought I had used what they called back in those days a cheat sheet. One accused me of having my answers be almost verbatim with the book. I told him that's the way I remembered it, I have a very good memory. I was in the first chair in front of his desk and he knew I didn't cheat. I challenged him to ask me questions right then. I had another professor who lost his tenure because of the way he treated me. A teacher called me "Nigger," and I got called that so much down there that I thought it was my middle name. Anyway I went right to the president and coach Luther and told them what he said. He denied it, but the classroom told them that this is what he called me, and he lost his tenure because of it.

There was also a situation that almost saw Johnson leave Murray.

I kept getting anonymous phone calls. I knew what it was about since I was the only brother on campus. I got a call one night and they said look out your window. I looked out and there was a four-foot cross burning outside it. This was 1962. I didn't know how to react. I called my Mom and in less than ten hours they were down there. My mom was a religious person and was praying for everyone. I'm not sure what magic words the coach said to my parents, but I stayed and continued my career there.

Despite everything Johnson went through, he bravely made sure he didn't forget about the struggle of African Americans and became part of the civil rights efforts.

The NAACP had gotten in contact with me and a few other Black players who were enrolling in all-white schools. They had this thing called SNCC, the Student Nonviolent Coordinating Committee, and we had to go down and practice things like sitting at a counter where they had people come at us and pour stuff on our head. Call you a bunch of names. It was all about not reacting. Unfortunately, I found it very difficult to do. When I spoke with Reverend Jesse Jackson, who said I was not entirely with the program, I said "Well, you have to understand Reverend Jackson. You, Dr. King and all these other young boys live in the South. You know how far you can go and can't. I was born up North and we did have de facto segregation, but it wasn't as blatant as this and we handled our own problems. I'm just not used to someone spitting in my face." They mentored me and then I had less problems with my teammates, although I still had problems with our opponents.

Years later, he had the chance to address his daughter Precious's team at Duquesne University through a Zoom call, and the subject of civil rights came up. He emotionally recalled the following: "I explained to them how much my heart was hurting and I said sixty years ago I was like you, I was marching, I was protesting with Dr. King and all these civil rights people and we sacrificed so much and we carried the scars in our head. It hurts me so much that 60 years later I have to see my baby [Precious] going through the same thing." He went on to say to the team, "Please forgive us, obviously we didn't do it right sixty years ago. But now that you know how things are, don't let it go any further."

Stewart fought through it all to have a phenomenal career at Murray State, where he was a two-time All–Ohio Valley Conference selection, scored 1,257 points in his career and helped the Racers to the 1963–64 conference title. He was captain in his senior season and eventually found his way to the Murray State Hall of Fame in 1979.

Stewart was selected by the New York Knicks in the third round of the 1966 NBA draft. Despite having an impressive preseason with the team and Coach Red Holzman telling him he made the team two days before the regular season began, Stewart ended up being cut. Stewart said that there was an unwritten policy that you had to have an equal number of Blacks as whites, because Blacks and whites didn't room together back then. The Knicks had an odd number of players. Stewart said to himself, "This is Murray State all over again." Cazzie Russell was the top pick and had a no-cut contract, so Stew was the odd man out and was cut.

He played in the Northern League before traveling to play professionally in Iceland. Soon the ABA was formed, and Johnson returned to the country and had a very successful career in the new circuit. In nine seasons with seven teams that included a stint back in Pittsburgh, Stewart had the ninth most points in league history (10,538). He also was the first player in the ABA to score over 60 points in a game, in 1971 with the Condors, when he scored 62 against the Floridians.

As Murray State looks to retire his number in the near future, Johnson still does not always look back fondly at his playing days at the school.

> *I see all these others get their numbers retired and I think, I was the first Black there, the first to be all-conference. But God willing I'm going to get down to Murray next year. Sometimes you need closure. But sometimes I have very negative feelings about my experiences down there. Even when people are patting me on the back about my achievements. I had them because I really never got the chance to enjoy my college life. Always looking over my shoulder.*

His role as a pioneer will always be something he's proud of.

> *I'm not sure if proud is the right word, but I am thankful I was in that situation. I had the prayers of my mom and dad to keep me safe. Sometimes when you're going through an experience you don't realize what you're going through, you just have to get through it. You have to get away from it to digest what really happened. In a way I can use the word proud. I'm*

looking at Murray College, I look at the Grizzlies' Ja Morant and every one that came after me that went to the NBA from Murray and I'm like "yea," so I am proud of that.

III
FOOTBALL

15

THE DOCTOR FROM WASHINGTON & JEFFERSON IS IN...THE RECORD BOOKS

By Tom Rooney

Linda West Nickens grew up in the home that was also the office of her father's general medical practice in Washington, D.C. Dr. Charles West operated that family-oriented practice for over five decades. Originally, his family and the practice were housed in nearby Alexandria, Virginia. But Dr. West found life in Virginia a quagmire of racial inequities in schools, businesses and, most important to him, medical facilities. Things could be so bad in Virginia that Black people wouldn't even be admitted to most hospitals. Dr. West delivered babies in his own office and in the homes of his patients. These were the lives and times of Black people in the mid-twentieth century. His patients beamed when they first met Charles West. They were so proud to have one of their own, a Black man, to protect them and to give them support at a time when not everyone could pay in cash. Sometimes, it was the "chicken and/or the eggs" as compensation instead of greenbacks.

From time to time, Linda would hear her mother prod her husband about "writing those things down so they're not lost to history." Dr. West would stop what he was doing, take a few minutes away from worrying about his patients and make some notes that thankfully survive today.

Who knew? Certainly, his patients and neighbors did not. Dr. Charles "Charlie" West was a major figure in college sports history when it came to breaking racial barriers. In 1922, playing for little Washington & Jefferson College in "Little Washington," Pennsylvania, he was the first Black

This is the historical marker commemorating the fact that Charles West was the first African American to play quarterback in the Rose Bowl, leading the Washington & Jefferson Presidents to a memorable 0–0 tie against the heavily favored University of California Golden Bears. Below is author Tom Rooney, who wrote the story of West for this book. *Courtesy of Tom Rooney.*

quarterback in the "granddaddy of them all," the Rose Bowl, in faraway Pasadena, California.

Not even the West children were really aware. "He was Dr. West and daddy. We were quiet kids. Living above the doctor's office, we were reminded as kids not to make a lot noise that might be typical of a young household," Linda said. "It really wasn't until much later we appreciated that the man we as a family and as a community loved for his care and dedication, in fact, was an important figure in something entirely different."

Yes, Charles West accomplished something on that January 2, 1922, that was notable then and even more praiseworthy now. West took the West by storm when he embarked with his team on Christmas Eve to begin a four-day train ride from western Pennsylvania to California and that date with destiny.

Only the most serious college football fans likely know that schools such as Washington & Jefferson (W&J) and two other Pittsburgh area institutions, Duquesne and Carnegie Tech (now Carnegie Mellon), competed at the highest level. The Ivy League schools, too, were in the gridiron upper echelon. And W&J's history incudes some names that resonate with college football lore, such as legendary coaches Greasy Neale and John Heisman, the latter whose name is connected with college football's most prestigious individual player award.

West grew up on a farm in Burgettstown, Pennsylvania, not far down the coal trucks road east of Washington, Pennsylvania. Racial taunts came early and often, but they did deter the young man. From those notes that survived, of his children he wrote: "My ambition was not just to run, tackle, punt or catch a football, my thoughts were as high as the moon. I wanted to win the approval of mankind and the only only if I won that could be achieved to win my own self-approval. I did not mind the name calling, it only spurred me on and I knew they were only belittling themselves."

From high school, it was on to a great college career. West led that undefeated 1921 W&J squad to a stellar season that included victories against Pitt, West Virginia and Syracuse. W&J was invited to take the cross-country rail trip to play the University of California on the day after New Year's in an event originally known as the East-West Football at Tournament Park in Pasadena. One day short of two full decades earlier, on January 1, 1901, the University of Michigan defeated Stanford, 49–0, in the inaugural edition.

A game earlier in that spectacular 1921 season, in Morgantown against WVU, was a test on and off the gridiron for young Charlie West. Drawing from those famous notes left to West's heirs, Dr. Arthur P. Davis of Howard University, who was also an author, wrote the following in an unpublished article in 1981 he titled "By-Passed Star." W&J was already 8-0 in the late fall in 1921 and had just come off a big win against powerful Pitt.

On November 24, 1921, when the train, bringing the Washington and Jefferson football team to play the University of West Virginia, pulled into Morgantown, there was an "official reception committee" waiting to greet the team; or to be more precise, to greet one man on the team. The townspeople on the committee knew that one of the stars on W and J was a Negro named West, and they came to give the presumptuous black man the kind of reception. They did not know, however, that Charles West was a light-colored Negro, one light enough to pass for white.

Dr. Davis quoted West: "I was the last man to leave the train and when I stepped off, the puzzled crowd yelled 'Where's the nigger?' I just smiled and said, 'We didn't bring him on this trip.'"

This is the house that Dr. Charles West practiced medicine in for over fifty years after his football career at W&J. *Courtesy of Tom Rooney.*

During the game, when the crowd discovered that West had fooled them, "Kill the nigger" yells cascaded from the stands. West more than endured. He led the W&J to a 13–0 win, one of six shutouts and ultimately a 10-0 record that saw his team outscore their opponents, 222–33.

With events like the game against WVU behind them, the team with the nickname Presidents faced a different kind of dishonor when they prepared for the West Coast: a lack of respect. In Vince Guerrieri's article "Date with Destiny" in a 2021 edition of *Pittsburgh Quarterly* ahead of the centennial of the game, he quoted Jack James of the *San Francisco Examiner* as saying, "All anyone 'west of the Mississippi' knew about W&J 'is confined in one simple, salient fact: They're both dead!'" Fans of Cal were equally flippant about the opponents. The morning of the game, a fan confronted W&J coach Neale, predicting a 14-point victory. "Listen," Neale responded, as quoted in a story thirty years later in *Colliers* magazine, "California couldn't score 14 points against this team if they started now and played until it got dark."

Nobody scored 14 points, it turned out. In fact, nobody scored any points at all!

The teams battled to a 0–0 tie. Well, W&J did appear to score a touchdown, but it was nullified by what seemed to its boosters as a little "home cooking" from the officials. Writer James ate some crow that put a large damper on the practitioners of Jim Crow back East, when he gave W&J their due. "A truly remarkable effort from a little college in western Pennsylvania that came across the continent and accomplished a feat that numerous institutions ten times their enrollment and treble their athletic reputation have found impossible," James wrote after the game.

The fanfare for that achievement did not particularly resonate through the decades, unless there was an anniversary, such as the centennial of the event in 2022. But the West family maintained a constant reminder of West's role and the "West Virginia Incident." It turns out that after the game in Morgantown, Charlie West took a little stroll through downtown. Many of the local stores had items in their windows celebrating the game. In the Davis article, he wrote:

> *The most colorful of these displays was one that which Frank Connors, a local druggist, had in his window. Its center attraction was a toy ambulance in which there was a Sambo-type doll, bearing a tag with WEST written on it. The display symbolized the hopes of the townspeople, that after their team had given the black player what he deserved, he would have left town in an ambulance. Charlie West had seen Connor's window, and after the game, he walked into the store and said to the proprietor: "I would like to have that ambulance and that caricature of me as a souvenir when you take down that display." Impressed by West's good-natured overlooking of the racial slur which the display intended, Mr. Connors gave West the whole business.*

The artifacts of that display were in the living room of Charles and LaVerne West's home in Washington, D.C., for decades and were a starting point for a lot of discussions about race relations. Linda West Nickens inherited them from her parents. "They're right on my mantel," she said from her home in Alexandria, Virginia. She is happy to tell the stories, the ones her mother prodded her father to write down in the precious breaks in the doctor's busy day. "My dad was always even tempered, even in situations like that Saturday in Morgantown," she said. "He'd be surprised but a little pleased too with all this attention about something that happened so many years ago."

16

WESTERN PENNSYLVANIA'S GIFT TO THE BIG TEN

WILLIE THROWER AND SANDY STEPHENS

By David Finoli

There are many inspirational stories of integration in college football, including that of the Big Ten Conference. Perhaps two of the greatest stories came as gifts from western Pennsylvania: Michigan State quarterback Willie Thrower from New Kensington, and an All-American signal caller from Minnesota who came to the Gophers via Uniontown, Sandy Stephens. Both are often forgotten for their achievements, but both made an incredible impact on the integration of college football and, in the case of Thrower, on the professional version of the game, as he was the Jackie Robinson of the league when it came to quarterbacks.

From the same high school that produced Olympic gold medalist John Woodruff, Stephens was an excellent quarterback for Uniontown. He led them to an 8-2 mark his senior season, but unfortunately the Asian flu cost them a game against Baldwin. The cancellation left them with not enough Gardner points, which is a system the WPIAL uses, awarding points based on a team's opponents' record and margin of victory when determining playoff tiebreakers. Stephens explained in an article on the Fayette County Hall of Fame website, "The Asiatic flu was the real reason that we missed out. We didn't get a chance to play Baldwin and they were a good team and we would have had enough points. We would have been first or second had we been able to play them but we missed Baldwin and Redstone Twp. We made up the Redstone game at the end of the season but we couldn't make up Baldwin so that made us third in the Gardner race."

Stephens received fifty offers to play major college football. A fine all-around athlete, he also had six NCAA basketball scholarship offers and interest from the hometown Pittsburgh Pirates. He eventually chose the University of Minnesota, feeling he had his best chance to play quarterback there. He went there with his friend from Clairton, Judge Dickson, who doubled as fullback and linebacker, and the two had dreams of taking the Gophers to places they had never been before.

Dickson recalled in an article on the Gophers' official athletic website:

> We dreamed of going to the Rose Bowl. When we got to Minnesota, Sandy put a picture of the Rose Bowl up on the wall and one of our teammates came into our room one night and he started laughing and he said "What's that?" And I remember Sandy saying "It's the Rose Bowl" and he said "Why do you have it on your wall?" And Sandy said "Because we're going," and he laughed some more and said, "What makes you think you're going?" Sandy said, "because we have guys like us that can make it happen. We have to believe we're gonna get there and we can do it."

After a 2-7 campaign his first year, Stephens, the first Black quarterback in Minnesota history, did just that. He was a major part of their national championship squad in 1960 and a year later helped give the Gophers their lone Rose Bowl win with a performance that garnered him a spot in the game's Hall of Fame. He also made his most important mark on the integration of sports in this country, becoming the first Black player to be named a First-Team All-American at quarterback. His talent was special, but so was his leadership. According Dickson, "I do know this: It was Sandy Stephens, more than anyone, who proved that black and white players could come together behind a black quarterback and win."

After his career was over for the Gophers, he never had much of a professional career. A car accident hurt his chances in the NFL, although he did get the chance to play for the Montreal Alouettes in the Canadian Football League. While Willie Thrower was not the talent Stephens was with Minnesota, he is a very essential figure in the history of sports integration in the country.

Coming out of New Kensington, where he was an All-American his senior season in high school and led his team to two Class AA titles, Thrower was recruited to Michigan State in 1949 by then assistant coach Duffy Daugherty, who eventually became a Hall of Fame head coach with the Spartans. While he played sparingly his first two seasons in 1950 and 1951, the fact that he made it onto the gridiron made history, as Thrower was the first Black quarterback in Big Ten history. Considered the best natural passer on the team, Thrower had his best season in a Michigan State uniform his senior season while helping to lead the Spartans to a national championship.

That year, Thrower split the position with All-American Tom Yewcic, who acknowledged in an article on the Michigan State athletic website that Willie was in fact the best passer they had. It was said that he had the ability to throw a pass accurately 60 yards downfield at a time when that was an unusual feat. In a rout against Texas A&M, he tossed a 53-yard TD pass on his first throw, one unfortunately called back on an offside penalty. But he then led the Spartans to their final two scores. He ended up completing 59 percent of his passes for the season for 400 yards and 5 touchdowns.

Even though there was never a time during his career in East Lansing when he was a starter, it was apparent that Willie Thrower had one of the best passing abilities in college football. He was signed to a one-year NFL contract in 1953 by George Halas and the Chicago Bears. On October 19, 1953, he had his second Jackie Robinson moment, this one a great deal more important. He became the first African American to play quarterback in the NFL.

Starter George Blanda was struggling against the San Francisco 49ers, as Thrower recalled in the same Michigan State website article.

> *I got into the San Francisco game after (Bears coach) George Halas got dissatisfied with (starting quarterback) George Blanda. He (Halas) jumped up and said "Willie, Willie, warm up, get in there." So I warmed up, went in, and took them from our own 40-yard line all the way down to about the 15. All of a sudden, he sends George back in, and the fans, boy they really jumped on him, (saying) "leave Willie in, leave Willie in."*

With his entrance into the contest, Thrower found a place in history as the first Black quarterback in the NFL.

After the game, Halas was left to explain his decision to reinsert Blanda for Thrower. In an article in the *Chicago Tribune* on October 20, 1953, Halas said, "We had a particular play we wanted called in that situation and Thrower, who has not yet learned all our offense, did not know it."

Thrower would play in only one more game in his NFL career before moving on to the CFL, where his career ended at the age of twenty-seven due to a shoulder injury. Despite the fact that his pro career was not successful, Willie was proud of his place in history. "I look at it like this: I was like the Jackie Robinson of football. A black quarterback was unheard of before I hit the pros."

It would be fifteen years before another Black quarterback played in the NFL, indicating just how unique Willie Thrower's moment in history was. He and Stephens had careers to be celebrated. They were western Pennsylvania's gifts to the Big Ten and the NFL.

17

A TEMPORARY INTEGRATION

THE STORY OF RAY KEMP

By David Finoli

Integration in sports had a usual sequence of events. First, there was a tough time convincing owners or college presidents that signing Black athletes was the correct thing to do both socially and from a competitive standpoint. Then, it was a time of obstacles for the pioneering athletes as, little by little, acceptance came and more Black athletes were signed. While this sequence was the most common one, in the NFL, it unfortunately happened somewhat backward. Such was the case for the first Black player to take the field for the Pittsburgh Steelers (then called the Pirates), Ray Kemp.

Born in Cecil, Pennsylvania, Kemp was not only a great player on his high school team but also played the saxophone and worked in the coal mines. After slate smashed his foot in the mines, his high school football coach (and also a doctor), according to Kemp in a *New York Times* article on January 11, 1998, said to the young star: "Ray, what are you doing in the coal mine? You could have a career in college football. I'm afraid if you're not careful you'll ruin it." Ray didn't have to be told twice, so he quit the mines and eventually enrolled at Duquesne University under famed coach Elmer Layden. Kemp said that when he began, he noticed only two other Black players; both were gone after his first season.

Kemp had troubles when he started. When it looked like he was about to be cut from the team, the Dukes line coach suggested a move to tackle. It was the perfect suggestion, and Kemp became a star on the Bluff. Eventually,

This is a statue dedicated to Steelers owner Art Rooney, "The Chief," that stands outside of Acrisure Stadium. Rooney was responsible for bringing Ray Kemp to the Pirates (Steelers) in 1933 as their first African American player. *Courtesy of David Finoli.*

he became an Honorable Mention All-American and received both his bachelor's degree and master's at the school. It was at his football banquet following his senior campaign that his opportunity to play professional football came about. It was there that a conversation with Art Rooney opened the doors.

In an article about Kemp on the website Profootballhof.com, Ray stated, "Art Rooney came up to me at our athletic banquet following my senior year at Duquesne and told me that he would like me to play for his JP Rooney semi-pro team if I was going to stay around Pittsburgh." While the All-American tackle decided to go to graduate school at Duquesne and serve as Layden's line coach, he also chose to play for Rooney's squad as the lone African American on the team. (He also played for a team in Erie as its only Black player.)

The JP Rooneys were one of the area's preeminent semipro teams, and when Pennsylvania voted to end the Blue Laws in 1933, Rooney took his team to the National Football League and formed the Pittsburgh Pirates (eventually renamed the Steelers). The Blue Laws were an attempt by government to force families to honor Sunday as the "Lord's Day" for prayer and rest. The laws made it illegal to play baseball or football on Sundays. Most of Rooney's squad would come from the JP Rooneys, including Kemp, making him the first African American to play for the franchise.

The *Pittsburgh Courier* was thrilled that the Cecil native would be playing for the team. An August 26, 1933 article stated: "The acquisition of the big, bounding Duke tackle would certainly be an asset to the team. Kemp rated as one of the best tackles ever produced in this section and named on the Associated Press All American teams for Honorable Mention in '29 has a large following here and his presence in the lineup would do much to draw out many admirers of both races."

The team debuted against the New York Giants on September 20, 1933, at Forbes Field. While Kemp wasn't listed in the starting lineup, he in fact did start and reportedly was arguably the most impressive Pirate on the field during the 23–2 loss. According to a September 30 story in the *Pittsburgh Courier*, after trying to run toward Kemp, "four attempts were enough to convince them that Elmer Layden of the original Four Horsemen, and his staff of Duquesne coaches all couldn't be wrong. From then on the visiting backs allowed a decided preference for the other side of the Pirate forward wall."

In his interview on the Pro Football Hall of Fame website, Kemp remembered getting a loud ovation as he took the field. He also recalled what could have been a play to remember: "I had my hands taped heavily because that's what we did as linemen. On about the third or fourth play I was in. I broke through and their passer threw the ball right into my hands, but I couldn't hold it because of the tape." He also recalled that some of his fellow Pirates criticized his stand-up style of play. He told Layden about his teammates' issues with him, and his college coach assured him, "They are crazy Ray. I saw the game and you were tremendous."

Unfortunately, the beginning of Kemp's career would last just two more games before Rooney released him. According to the *Courier*, it was a "big surprise to local sportsdom." Rooney claimed it was a temporary release, as he cut Kemp and six others to reduce the roster to twenty-two players.

By all accounts, Kemp had been one of the strongest players on the team at the time and was reportedly upset by the decision. He told the paper that "rather than be temporarily suspended he would quit altogether." Rooney, "The Chief," had stated in the *Pittsburgh Courier* article on October 14, 1933, that "we had no fault to find with Kemp's playing ability but he was a 'sub' and not a 'regular'," claiming that coach Jap Douds kept other men with pro experience over him, although it was also reported that the relationship between Kemp and Douds was strained. In the article on the Pro Football Hall of Fame website, the Cecil native recalled Rooney telling him: "Ray, I feel you are as good a ball player as we have on the club but I am not going over the head of the coach. You know how I feel about you personally." Kemp claimed further that Douds had some buddies on the team whom he decided to keep instead of Kemp.

Eventually, it did turn out to be temporary. Kemp was reinstated for the last couple of games of the season, including a trip to New York to play the Giants. On that trip, he was asked to stay at a Harlem YMCA instead of the team hotel, which claimed it didn't have room for him.

It was a tough season, and Kemp was not asked to return in 1934. In fact, the only other African American in the league, Joe Lilliard, a running back with the Chicago Cardinals, was also cut following the season. The owners at that point had forgotten about integration, as there were no Black NFL players in the league for twelve more seasons until the NFL was reintegrated in 1946. The Steelers did not have an African American on their roster for nineteen years. The team signed seven Black players in the preseason before the 1952 campaign, with only Jack Spinks making the Opening Day roster and reintegrating the Steelers.

For Kemp, while he didn't play again in the NFL, he had a great career that included a head coaching stint at Bluefield State College, where he went 8-0-1 in his first season, 1934. He also coached basketball and track and held positions in athletic administration at Lincoln University and Tennessee State, where he coached Olympic gold medal long jumper Ralph Boston.

Kemp ended up being the last surviving member of that first Steeler team in 1933 and stayed a fan of the franchise, even showing up at Three Rivers Stadium in 1982 as the franchise celebrated the fiftieth anniversary of that squad. He is often a forgotten pioneer but, no doubt about it, an important part of the franchise's history.

18

A SAVIOR FOR THE CITY

JIMMY JOE ROBINSON

By David Finoli

When Jimmy Joe Robinson came to the University of Pittsburgh in 1945 as the first African American player in the school's storied football program, it wasn't met with the firestorm that Jackie Robinson would endure when he signed his historic contract with the Brooklyn Dodgers later that fall. In fact, the *Pittsburgh Sun-Telegraph* received letters challenging the fact that he was the first African American to play for the Panthers (he was). His incredible talent was on display many times during his career at Pitt, but it was a moment twenty years later with which he made his mark on the city.

Coming out of Connellsville High School, Robinson was an incredible all-around athlete. He was All-WPIAL (Western Pennsylvania Interscholastic Athletic League) and captured titles in the long jump and the 220-yard and 440-yard dashes in the Allegheny County Independent Districts Title Meet his senior year. In basketball, he lettered and was offered a scholarship by Westminster College. But football was where Jimmy Joe truly thrived.

According to his son James Robinson Jr. in his book about his father, *They Call Me Jimmy Joe*, the Connellsville native ran for over 1,500 yards with 16 touchdowns while being named to the All-State squad. The younger Robinson quoted his dad in the book: "Football was where I wanted to be, but in those days, coming out of Connellsville, and having never been anywhere, I never thought that I'd go to college. In fact, I had looked forward to working on the railroad with the rest of my friends. No colleges ever wrote

Jimmy Joe Robinson was the first African American to play in the University of Pittsburgh football program. An exciting running back who thrilled fans with his speed, Robinson perhaps had his greatest impact as a reverend, helping keep violence to a minimum in the city after Martin Luther King was killed in 1968. *Courtesy of the University of Pittsburgh Athletics.*

me letters, colleges weren't requiring black athletes at that time." Luckily for the elder Robinson, Clark Shaughnessy, the head coach at the University of Pittsburgh, was interested in looking to add talent at Pitt regardless of race.

While Robinson was surprised at the attention the Panthers' coaching staff was giving him, sending two coaches to his house to recruit and sign him to play for Pitt, he and his family were thrilled for the opportunity to continue his football career.

As mentioned earlier in the chapter, there was not a media controversy like that Jackie Robinson endured during the same period. In an editorial in the June 14, 1945 *Pittsburgh Sun-Telegraph*, sports editor Harry Keck stated that he

> *noticed that Pitt, for the first time has a Negro player trying out for its football squad, one Jimmy Joe Robinson, a freshman from Connellsville.*
>
> *It is remarkable that the Panthers haven't given the colored lads a chance to make the team before. There are many of them in the Western Conference and on the Pacific Coast and Cornell University has had its share of them and now boasts a stellar Negro player in Paul Robeson Jr. a fine end who will be transformed into a halfback next fall....*
>
> *You'll find more than a few Negro stars on All-American rosters down through the years.*
>
> *Pitt has had its share of Negro stars, most notably Johnny Woodruff and Everett Utterback, on its track teams. It never has had had them in baseball, football or basketball. It plays against Negroes in football so why shouldn't it avail itself of any who are good enough to make the team?*

Shaughnessy was adamant about recruiting the best players regardless of race. Westinghouse High School's Allen Carter and Herb Douglas from Allderdice joined Robinson on the squad. Douglas was so confident in his abilities that he secured Red Grange's number 77 for Pitt. He eventually achieved greater things on the track by capturing the bronze medal in the long jump at the 1948 London Summer Olympic Games. It was Robinson, though, who secured the starting spot at left-halfback. Keck noted in the opening 20–0 victory against WVU that Robinson stood out.

He proved to be every bit as impressive as Shaughnessy had hoped his freshman year, the highlight of which was a 90-yard punt return in the season finale against Penn State that was the difference in a 7–0 upset victory by the Panthers. The play remains a school record. He also led the team in rushing with 273 yards.

After spending seven months in the army in 1946, Jimmy Joe returned to school in 1947, as Mike Milligan had replaced Shaughnessy as head coach. Milligan switched the offense from the T-formation to the single wing, which disappointed the talented running back. In the book by his son, Jimmy is quoted as saying: "Although we ran the single wing in high school, the T-formation was more to my liking, more suitable to my talents, going back to the single wing was not my forte. Boy did I miss Shaughnessy."

While not happy in the single wing, he still made several impressive plays over the next three seasons, including a kickoff return of 100 yards against Purdue and an 85-yard punt return versus Michigan State. He ended up having a fine career with Pitt, although he did experience prejudice along the way, including not being served at some restaurants, not being allowed to stay at certain hotels and being held back against some southern schools. What Robinson did find out, though, was that his teammates supported him through the issues, including on a trip to Purdue, where the squad voted to stay in the school's student union instead of a more comfortable hotel because the hotels would admit only the white players.

After completing his career with the Panthers, Jimmy Joe was drafted by the Cleveland Browns. Unfortunately, he was once again drafted into the army, where he spent three years. He was stationed at Fort Myers in Virginia and spent his time in the military playing football. He did so thanks to Steeler running back Fran Rogel, who suggested that Robinson tell the officers he was a draft pick of the Browns. The halfback concluded in his biography, "It was good to mention the Browns because if I hadn't, they would have shipped me right to Korea."

Instead, he played football during his two-and-a-half-year army stint, and when he was released, he attempted to revive his career with Cleveland. Unfortunately, in the middle of an exciting run that looked like it was going for a touchdown, he pulled his hamstring. The injury was worse than feared, and head coach Paul Brown was not a man who was patient waiting for an injured player to heal. He traded Jimmy Joe to the Steelers, and Pittsburgh asked him to play a position other than halfback. Halfback was all Robinson knew, and he didn't want to embarrass himself playing another position.

He never saw the field after that and eventually signed with the Montreal Alouettes. It was there that his wife, Betty, a woman who was very outgoing compared to Jimmy, who had more of a quiet nature, found God. Eventually, Robinson also found his faith. In his son's book, the talented halfback speaks of that moment. "It's hard to describe, but the spirit of the Lord hit me like a bolt of lightning. I couldn't run and hide any more. I knew he was calling me. I ran to him and I never looked back."

He attended the Pittsburgh Theological Seminary in 1957, the same time that Fred Rogers (later "Mr. Rogers") attended, and graduated two years later. The next chapter of Robinson's life began and, with it, opportunities to make a greater impact on the city than he had as a player on the Pitt football team.

In 1964, he agreed to travel to Greenwood, Mississippi, to help Blacks get out to vote. He found himself embroiled in the civil rights movement headed by Dr. Martin Luther King and was thrown in a Greenwood jail for protesting. In his biography, he stated: "The last thing I wanted was to get arrested in Greenwood, Mississippi. I wanted the hell out but sure enough we were tossed into paddy wagons. They opened the doors to this big bus, grabbed us by the arm and threw us on the bus. I made sure I jumped in so I wouldn't be thrown in. They actually segregated us, they put us on two different busses by race. Also Blacks were shipped off to one jail, whites to another. We got there, did mug shots and were put in a holding cell." While he may not have wanted to be in the middle of the civil rights violence, he put himself there on several occasions as this was not the only time he was arrested for protesting.

By 1968, Robinson was heading a church in the Manchester section of the city. When King was assassinated, violence was brewing across the country. Robinson helped to reduce the violence in the city by working with the community to build a basketball court in a warehouse while providing youth with food, radio and TV to help give them options other than confrontations with the police. The youth and church members worked up to ten shifts a day to keep things going at the warehouse until eventually the tensions subsided.

It was Robinson's efforts with the church that had a more lasting impact on Pittsburgh than anything he did on the gridiron. He did much more afterward, including organizing a gang summit in 1994, when violence was erupting around Pittsburgh.

Even though Jimmy Joe Robinson is still an important figure at the University of Pittsburgh, it was his life afterward by which he was a true savior to the city.

19

PREJUDICE OFF THE FIELD....AND PERHAPS ON IT

BOBBY GRIER AT THE SUGAR BOWL

By David Finoli

Bobby Grier was put in history's road as a pioneer, becoming the first African American to play in a Sugar Bowl contest. While he wasn't looking for the spotlight, he held himself up proudly with all he had to endure in making his memorable appearance. There was one thing he couldn't defeat, though: a referee who made a phantom pass-interference call against Grier that turned out to be the deciding moment in a 7–0 victory by the Georgia Tech Yellow Jackets. Was it a call filled with prejudice, or just a poor one?

Grier came to the Panthers from the legendary high school in Massillon, Ohio, where the Pitt fullback recalled that they had won four or five consecutive state titles at the time he played in the early to mid-1950s. He was recruited by several major colleges, including Miami (Ohio) and UCLA, the school where Jackie Robinson excelled on the gridiron, but chose to join the Panthers. Playing for first-year coach John Michelosen, Pitt began the 1955 season with an impressive 27–7 victory over California, a game in which Grier excelled.

In an interview for a book I did along with Chris Fletcher, *Steel City Gridirons*, the Panther fullback said that he thought the best game of his career at Pitt was against California in the season opener. "I had quite a few yards in that game." After tough losses to Oklahoma, Navy and Miami (Florida), Pitt finished the season by taking on number six West Virginia and Penn State. A contingent from the Sugar Bowl came to Pitt Stadium against WVU with

Bobby Grier was a fine University of Pittsburgh running back who made history as the first Black player to play in the Sugar Bowl. Despite having to deal the a prejudice that was still a major factor in the South, he played a fine game, except for what appeared to be a phantom pass interference call against him that led to the only score in a 7–0 Georgia Tech victory. *Courtesy of the University of Pittsburgh Athletics.*

the intent of inviting the Mountaineers to New Orleans after their expected victory. The Panthers ended up upsetting West Virginia, 26–7, and then shut out Penn State, 20–0, to end the season at 7-3. They ended up ranked eleventh in the Associated Press poll while capturing the Lambert Trophy, emblematic of the best college football program in the East. The Panthers were rewarded with a bid to the Sugar Bowl against Georgia Tech, but this resulted in controversy, as Pitt had an African American on its roster in a game in which no Black football player had ever participated. Grier had hurt his knee during the season and had been benched at times by the first-year coach. Because of that, many white southerners hoped he would not play. It turned out that he did.

While by 1955 African Americans saw some doors opening for them, in the South, the civil rights movement seemed to be moving at a snail's pace. In 1954, the *Brown v. Board of Education* decision by the Supreme Court frustrated many southern schools, and in the months preceding the Sugar Bowl, Emmett Till had been hanged in Mississippi and Rosa Parks was arrested for not sitting in the back of a bus. In the past, teams invited to the Sugar Bowl with African American players were not permitted to play those players. They were limited to watching their teammates from the press box and not allowed to practice or stay in the same hotel as the white players. The University of Pittsburgh was not interested in going to a game in which Grier wasn't permitted to play, so it made sure it had assurances from the Sugar Bowl committee that Bobby would be allowed to participate. Pitt also wanted a ten-thousand-seat section of Tulane Stadium in New Orleans for the Pitt contingent, one reserved for whites only, to be desegregated. Before then, tickets included the stipulation that they were for Caucasian fans only. When Michelosen brought up the bid for a team vote, he exclaimed, according to an article by Johnny McGonigle on February 19, 2022, in the *Pittsburgh Post-Gazette*: "As you know, if we accept the bid, our teammate Bob would be the first black ever to play in the game, and this could set off fairly large political problems. You fellows have to decide what you want to do." Grier's teammate Bob Rosborough remembered in that same article that it took only two or three minutes to vote to go. They did so supporting Grier playing in the contest. Even though Pitt's demands were agreed to, Georgia governor Marvin Griffin was incensed and didn't want a school from his state to be forced to play a game against a Black player.

Grier was now involved in a controversy he didn't want to be part of, but Griffin made it tough on him. Grier would have surprising allies supporting him along with his teammates and his university.

According to a quote in a December 21, 2021 article on History.com, Griffin exclaimed: "No matter how much the Supreme Court seeks to sugarcoat its bitter pill of tyranny [civil rights], the people of Georgia and the South will not swallow it. The South stands at Armageddon. The battle is joined. We cannot make the slightest concession to the enemy in this dark and lamentable hour of struggle." While Griffin assumed everyone from the school would follow suit, the students and the team from Georgia Tech wanted nothing to do with his proclamation.

Over 1,500 Georgia Tech students protested with signs such as "Impeach Griffin" and "To Hell with Griffin." Students at the University of Georgia joined the protest against the governor. Before that, they violently marched on the capital, ripping up parking meters and breaking windows. The board at Georgia Tech was not happy with the students' actions and stated that it still supported segregation. But the board voted 13-1 to accept the bid to play against the Panthers and Grier. It wasn't a moment that moved the world closer to ending segregation. Both Georgia Tech and Georgia announced a new rule starting in 1956 that their teams would not play against Black athletes before an integrated crowd in segregated states

Even though Michelosen warned the team and the fullback about the political repercussions, the Massillon native was still stunned. In the interview he gave for *Steel City Gridirons*, he exclaimed when talking about Griffin and his complaints: "I was shocked, everybody was shocked. The school was behind me though. My teammates were behind me and everybody here was behind me." The support meant so much to the Panther halfback as the team traveled south for its date with history.

After the political uproar began to subside, the two schools took the field on January 2, 1956. The scoring began and ended on a controversial series early in the game. After a first-quarter Pitt fumble gave Georgia Tech the ball at the Panther 32, quarterback Wade Mitchell faked a handoff and rolled to his right with future Robert Morris coach Joe Walton in pursuit. Mitchell launched a pass into the end zone over wide receiver Don Ellis's head. Grier was lying on the ground in front of him. Surprisingly, a flag was thrown for pass interference against Grier. There were some reasons to think that this wasn't a racial matter and that the call was correct.

Jack Sell, the *Pittsburgh Post-Gazette* writer, claimed in his article on January 3, 1956, that it was a "correct call as viewed from the press box." In later articles by Ivan Maisel for ESPN.com and McGonigal's abovementioned *Pittsburgh Post-Gazette* article, they both said that no one ever claimed that the call was racially motivated, McGonigal even pointed out that the back judge who threw the flag was from Pittsburgh and not the South. The ball was placed at the 1-yard line. A couple of plays later, the Yellow Jackets scored the only points of the contest in a 7–0 victory. Ellis even claimed in a quote in the book *Steel City Gridirons*: "I got behind him. Then when I turned around to look for the pass, he shoved me in the stomach knocking me off stride. It was a fine pass and I think I could have caught it."

The Panthers dominated the contest statistically from that point on, outgaining their opponents, 313–142. Pitt was stopped inside the Tech 10-yard line twice, at the end of each half. Grier went on to have a good game, running for a game-high 51 yards on 6 carries, but the game is remembered today for that one pass interference call. Despite his good game, Grier was upset at the play. "I was playing defensive halfback at the time. I felt a push on my back, and I fell down. The Georgia Tech receiver jumped for the ball and the pass went about three feet over his head and I was called for pass interference."

With Sell, an eyewitness to the play, saying it was a penalty on Grier and current writers saying that there has never been accusations of racism, what exactly happened? In the first place, saying that no one claimed racism is wrong. In my interview with the halfback, he said, "I think it was racially motivated but it's hard to tell." As far as the play being pass interference, in looking at the film of the play, Grier's description is correct. He was on the ground as Ellis was standing up as the ball flew over his head. It would be difficult to see any way that the play was pass interference. It's also impossible at this point to tell if the call was racially motivated, but just because the referee was from Pittsburgh doesn't mean it wasn't. You can't see the full play from the film, but if it actually was as bad as it looked at the end, the claim of racism can't be dismissed.

In the end, it wasn't the interference call that should be remembered but the brave effort of Bobby Grier to face racism in the segregated South in an attempt to open doors for those Black athletes who came after him.

20

THE FOUNDATION

JOE GREENE MADE THE STEELERS THE BIG, BAD STEELERS

By Chris Fletcher

Joe Greene is widely considered the greatest Steeler ever—high praise on a team that counts thirty-two Hall of Famers among its ranks, with at least three more on the horizon.

However, the early years of the Steelers were marked by poor teams made up of terrible players. From their first season in 1933 through to 1969—the year they selected Greene—the Steelers did not win a playoff game. Such poor results weren't accidental. There was a reason they were the league's lovable losers. Management sucked at talent evaluation and development.

The importance of the selection of Greene cannot be overstated in turning around the fortunes of a moribund franchise. First, he was the initial selection made by rookie head coach Chuck Noll. Prior to the draft, Noll had replaced Bill Austin, who posted a 2-11-1 record in 1968. (A bit of Steelers trivia: Austin is the last coach to be fired by the team.) It was imperative that a new era under Noll get off to a positive start. In the days before free agency, for the Steelers to join the NFL's elite, help would have to come primarily through the draft.

But Noll had some bad history to overcome. How bad was it? The pre-Noll draft years were as lean as a skinless chicken breast. The words *good* and *draft* were rarely used together in Pittsburgh, unless, of course, you were talking about a lovely beer with a creamy head poured in a local tavern.

Consider that this was the team that could have drafted Jim Brown, a generational talent at running back. Although it did select another NFL

The first draft pick in the Chuck Noll era, in 1969, was North Texas defensive lineman Joe Greene, shown walking off the field while in college. His number 75 is retired by both North Texas and the Pittsburgh Steelers, one of only three players in franchise history to be given that honor. *Courtesy of North Texas Athletics.*

Hall of Famer in that draft in quarterback Len Dawson, the Steelers cut him, allowing him to lead the Kansas City Chiefs to a Super Bowl win a few seasons later. Then there was the team's "historic" 1963 draft. The Steelers had no picks in the first *seven* rounds, having traded them all away to pick up a gaggle of veterans past their primes or players who would long one day to have a prime.

Given that abysmal record, few if any fans could have imagined the seismic shift that was to happen when it was announced that with their first pick, No. 4 overall, the Steelers selected six-foot, four-inch, 275-pound defensive lineman Joe Greene from tiny North Texas State.

The fans' reaction was largely, "Joe who?" Despite Greene being a consensus All-American, North Texas State wasn't exactly playing the Notre Dames, Michigans and Nebraskas of the world. He might have dominated in the college ranks, but there were questions about the level of opponents he was lining up against.

However, early on at training camp, Greene made believers out of his teammates during the annual Oklahoma drills. The practice technique developed by Oklahoma Sooners coach Bud Wilkinson matches a defensive lineman and an offensive lineman, and they face off. Greene was simply unstoppable, and he added a much-needed toughness to a team that had always hit hard. But Greene was also, well, green and raw. And he had a temper. Much of his anger was rooted in hating to lose. In fact, when he was notified of being drafted by the Steelers, Greene wasn't happy. The last thing he wanted to do was join a team with a forty-year history of losing.

It was a challenging rookie season for both Noll and Greene. The team opened the season with a 16–13 home win against the Detroit Lions. They dropped the remaining games, finishing 1-13. It was almost too much for the mercurial Greene. But he managed to win the NFL's Rookie of the Year Award. It also marked the first of Greene's team-record ten straight Pro Bowl selections.

The reclamation project was on, and Greene was the foundation on which to build it. Noll's teams would be predicated on having a physical, run-stopping defense, and Greene was the key. He presented a matchup problem the league hadn't seen before. He was strong. He was fast for his size and usually much quicker than the offensive linemen he was facing. He also revolutionized the position by lining up at an angle, with one shoulder pointing at the gap between two offensive linemen, rather than being square to the line of scrimmage. As a result, he drew double and triple teams (which he would routinely beat), allowing his teammates to make plays.

With Greene as the anchor and Noll mining other small historically Black colleges and universities for talent under the guidance of former *Pittsburgh Courier* sports editor Bill Nunn, who became a scout (see chapter 30), Pittsburgh became a legitimate contender in only three years. Had the

Joe Greene sits on the sidelines while playing for North Texas State University. Of note, Greene is drinking a Coca-Cola in the shot. He went on to make a Coke commercial while with the Steelers that became one of the most iconic ads ever made. *Courtesy of North Texas Athletics.*

"Greene experiment" not worked, it's unlikely the Steelers would have the head start they enjoyed against the rest of the league in drafting from that small-college pool.

In 1972, Greene led the young team to a playoff berth, something nearly unimaginable for Steelers nation. He was particularly unstoppable in a game against Houston, with the team thin on the defensive line because of injury. Greene took over the game, recording five sacks and recovering a fumble. It capped a season in which he was named Defensive Player of the Year.

Two years later, he won the award again, this time as a Super Bowl champion. Greene had an otherworldly postseason run. In the Super Bowl, he continually harassed Viking quarterback Fran Tarkenton and had an interception and a fumble recovery.

Greene would win three more Super Bowl titles, as his Steelers were the dominant team of the 1970s. He was a two-time Defensive Player of the Year. He was named to the NFL's all-time team. He also captured two more rings with the Steelers as part of the front office as a coach and talent evaluator in 2005 and 2008.

His talent allowed him to punch his own ticket to enshrinement in Canton, the first of the Steeler dynasty to be inducted (class of 1987). It's only fitting, since Greene was the one who started it all.

21

THE BALLAD OF JEFFERSON STREET JOE

By Chris Fletcher

Verse 1: Boom and It's Gone
It's 1974. My *Sports Illustrated* arrived today
On its cover "Pittsburgh's Black Quarterback"
As Joe Gilliam bombs the Colts
I marvel as he looks so cool
How did he get here?
From Tennessee State in Nashville, right off Jefferson Street that runs in front
Leading his team to a 21-1 record
Lighting up Eddie Robinson and Grambling
Even Bear Bryant praises his quick release: "Boom and it's gone," he muses
Throwing ropes, building hopes
An 11th round draft pick of the Steelers
This ain't no Terry Hanratty. Look out Terry Bradshaw, he's coming for you.

Verse 2: Beautiful Spirals
The '74 Steelers aren't quite right, not yet super
A team in transition, bounced hard from last year's playoffs
And there's a strike, but Jefferson Street Joe crosses the training camp picket lines
Coach Noll appreciates loyalty
He gives Joe a shot and he doesn't disappoint

Joe Gilliam, an immense talent at Tennessee State University, was drafted by the Pittsburgh Steelers in the eleventh round of the 1972 NFL draft. One of the first Black quarterbacks in the NFL, Joe earned the starting spot over Terry Bradshaw to begin the 1974 campaign and was magnificent in his first two contests. Eventually, Bradshaw took back his starting job, and Gilliam's life fell apart as a result of drug addiction. He was out of the NFL after only one more season. *Courtesy of Tennessee State University Athletics.*

New blood in Lynn Swann, John Stallworth, weapons to be sure
A quarterback's dream
Joe leads the team to an undefeated preseason
He beats out Bradshaw, told you he was gunning for you
Throwing ropes, building hopes
Airing it out all over the field
Beautiful spirals. This sure ain't no Terry Hanratty.

Chorus
That's the story of Jefferson Street Joe Gilliam
Pittsburgh's Black quarterback
He went from arm like a cannon
To cannon fodder and something sadder
A footnote in Steelers' history

Verse 3: Coach Noll and the Missed Field Goal
Joe bombed the Colts 30–0
Remember the cover legend in the making
But Coach Noll wanted to run the ball, control the clock
This was '74 and not today's pass-friendly game
Three things can happen on a pass and two of them are bad
Joe played a wide-open style, 50 passes in a 35–35 tie against the Broncos
Roy Gerela missed the field goal, or the team would be 2-0
But damn it, Joe, run the ball
This is your fault, and we need a change—where's the loyalty?
Throwing ropes, dashing hopes
After a humiliating home loss to the Raiders, Bradshaw's back
Thank God it's not Terry Hanratty

Verse 4: Racism in the Huddle?
Was the NFL and Pittsburgh ready for a Black quarterback?
The first African American quarterback to start a season since the merger
Now sits on the bench
Was it race? Joe thought so
The death threats told him so
"I thought if you played well, you got to play," he says
"I guess I didn't understand
The significance of being a Black quarterback at the time."
But defying Coach Noll was also significant and so many turnovers
No more throwing ropes, just fading hopes
Joe is benched
And even Terry Hanratty gets to play.

Chorus
That's the story of Jefferson Street Joe Gilliam
Pittsburgh's Black quarterback
He went from starting signal caller

To backup and free-faller
A footnote in Steelers' history

Verse 5: The Fall
The thing about meteors is that they fall fast
Joe had the talent, the physical gifts
Even Stallworth and Andy Russell said so
You can't cross Coach Noll
You can't ease the pain with cocaine, heroin and alcohol or Super Bowl rings
Gone from Pittsburgh in '76 and off to New Orleans, cut twice by the Saints
Arrested for possession of a gun and cocaine
A comeback with the Alabama Vulcans semi-pro team
Cut short when he steals the owner's car
Where's the hope? Just drug user tropes
Living in a cardboard box under a bridge for two years
Addiction is a curse, no smart-ass Terry Hanratty reference needed.

Verse 6: Partial Redemption
Joe didn't give up on himself or on football
In '83 he attempts to come back to pro football but not in Pittsburgh
The USFL gave him a shot
Cut by the Denver Gold, picked up by the Washington Federals
Four games started, five touchdowns and 10 interceptions
Working hard to keep clean and sober is a constant battle
Welcomed back to Pittsburgh, December 16, 2000,
For the last Steelers game at Three Rivers Stadium
The home for those olden frozen ropes and unfulfilled hopes
Joe basks in the cheers, waves to the crowd
But a little over a week later he's dead from an overdose alone on Christmas Day

Chorus
That's the story of Jefferson Street Joe Gilliam
Pittsburgh's Black quarterback
He went from arm like a cannon
To cannon fodder and something sadder
A tragic figure in Steelers' history

22

MIKE TOMLIN

THE SPIRIT OF THE RULE

By Josh Taylor

The history of coaching diversity in the National Football League is nearly as complicated in the early twenty-first century as it was during the one hundred years prior, marked by inconsistency among its ranks. After the hiring of Frederick Douglass "Fritz" Pollard by the Akron Pros as the league's first Black head coach in 1921, there wasn't another Black head coach until Art Shell with the Los Angeles Raiders in 1988. While the number of African American coaches has grown since Shell's hiring, the grand total sits at less than forty four decades later.

In January 2007, the NFL had five Black men patrolling the sidelines as head coaches. A sixth would be forthcoming with the Pittsburgh Steelers, an organization whose owner and president, Dan Rooney, had proposed a solution to a problem that was seeming to get worse before it got better. Five years before, the league saw dismissals of two African American head coaches who had been otherwise largely successful.

The Tampa Bay Buccaneers fired their head coach, Tony Dungy, after six seasons, four postseason appearances and an overall record of 54-42. The Minnesota Vikings had fired their longtime head coach, Dennis Green, after ten seasons, eight playoff appearances—including two in the NFC Championship Game—and a record of 97-62. The Vikings' 5-10 record in 2001 marked the first and only losing season of Green's tenure in Minnesota. Furthermore, after the debut of Fritz Pollard more than eighty years before,

Green and Dungy were two of only eleven minority head coaches who had been hired since then.

Soon after the dismissals of Dungy and Green were announced, two attorneys, Cyrus Mehri and Johnnie Cochran, published a study titled "Black Coaches in the National Football League: Superior Performance, Inferior Opportunities." The study summarized: "We believe that America's Game should represent America's diversity and the best values in our society." Among the study's findings, it was discovered that Black head coaches were less likely to be hired than their white colleagues and more likely to be fired, despite winning a higher percentage of regular-season games.

In light of Cochran and Mehri's findings, Rooney, then the chairman of the NFL's diversity committee, helped implement a rule that would ensure that minority coaches would be considered for head coaching positions. The rule was also supported by a group of minority scouts, coaches and other league personnel in addition to the players, of whom the majority are African American. In 2003, the "Rooney Rule" was implemented in the league, and by 2006, the overall percentage of African American coaches had increased to 22 percent, up from 6 percent before the rule went into effect three years before.

As the 2006 season came to a close, the Steelers finished with a record of 8-8, missing out on the playoffs for the second time in four seasons. Head coach Bill Cowher resigned on January 5, 2007, after fifteen years of leading the Steelers to an overall record of 161-99-1, ten playoff appearances, two Super Bowl appearances and one championship title. As the search began for Cowher's replacement, the list of candidates featured internal candidates such as offensive coordinator Ken Whisenhunt and offensive line coach Russ Grimm. Chicago Bears defensive coordinator Ron Rivera, of Puerto Rican and Mexican descent, had also been interviewed for the job, satisfying the minimum criterion of minority coaches considered under the Rooney Rule. But one more minority candidate remained, one who would change the course of the franchise's history.

Mike Tomlin, the defensive coordinator of the Minnesota Vikings, was given an interview by the Steelers for the vacant head coaching job. Tomlin, a former wide receiver at the College of William & Mary who had coached wide receivers and defensive backs at five different universities in the late 1990s, was hired by head coach Tony Dungy and the Tampa Bay Buccaneers to be their defensive backs coach before the 2001 season. During that time, Tomlin had become familiar with Dungy's 4-3 Cover Two scheme, which was adapted from the version Dungy learned as a player and assistant under former Steelers head coach Chuck Noll. It was later known as the "Tampa 2." After Dungy was fired by the Buccaneers following the 2001 season, the team carried on with the same defensive scheme, with Tomlin leading the defensive backs for four more seasons. In 2002, under new head coach Jon Gruden and retained defensive coordinator Monte Kiffin, the Buccaneers defense led the league with the fewest yards and points allowed on the way to a 12-4 record and a 48–21 win over the Oakland Raiders in Super Bowl XXXVII. During that game, the Bucs intercepted 5 passes off Raiders' quarterback Rich Gannon, 4 of which came from Tomlin's defensive backfield.

Before the 2006 season, Tomlin left Tampa to join new head coach Brad Childress in Minnesota as the Vikings' defensive coordinator. Despite a 6-10 record, Tomlin's defense ranked eighth in the league in total yards allowed, largely due to Minnesota having the league's top rushing defense. They were also third in the league with 36 takeaways. Despite only one year of coordinator experience, on January 21, 2007, the Steelers hired the thirty-four-year-old Tomlin as the sixteenth head coach in the franchise's history. Tomlin became the first Black man to be hired as head coach of the Steelers and the tenth hired in league history. While Tomlin's ethnicity bucked one trend within the Steelers organization, his age followed another: the previous three head coaches the team hired had all been defensive assistants younger than forty years of age.

"These are great football people," said Tomlin of the Steelers' front office, according to a story by the Associated Press. "I've got a great deal of respect for what they do and what they've done. It's just a very humbling experience to be involved in, but, at the same time, professional football is what I do and I'm a competitor like everyone else."

Perhaps fate intervened on that day in late January. On the same day the Steelers selected Tomlin, two of his colleagues—Dungy and Chicago Bears head coach Lovie Smith—had become the first two Black head coaches to reach the Super Bowl. Smith, like Tomlin, had been a defensive assistant under Dungy in Tampa before being named head coach by the Bears in 2004. Steelers president Art Rooney II called Tomlin to offer him the position while watching both of his friends advance past the conference championship round.

"He's a good coach, a great communicator and now he'll have a chance to show what he can do," Dungy told ESPN.com.

While having possibly benefited from the league rule that bore his owner's name, Tomlin gave no indication that the expectations placed on him would be any different than they would be for any other coach. "I think regardless of who they hire to be the head coach, they expect him to lead," said Tomlin at his introductory press conference. "Part of leading is being prepared to do things you feel strongly about. I'm no different from anyone else in that regard."

Tomlin would soon meet those expectations early as the Steelers won seven of their first nine games, including a 34–7 win over the rival Cleveland Browns in Week 1. The Steelers finished Tomlin's first season with a 10-6 record and clinched first place in the AFC North Division before a 31–29 loss to the Jacksonville Jaguars in the AFC Wild Card round of the playoffs. The following season, Tomlin led the Steelers to a 12-4 record, a second consecutive AFC North Division title and a 27–23 win over the Arizona Cardinals in Super Bowl XLIII, the team's second world championship in four seasons.

After fifteen seasons, Tomlin has accumulated a record of 154-85-2—a winning percentage of 64.3 percent, twentieth-best all-time—ten playoff appearances, seven division championships and two Super Bowl appearances with one championship. The Steelers' investment in Tomlin, like his two predecessors, Cowher and Noll, has paid off tremendously. The three men are the only head coaches hired by the organization in fifty-three seasons, yielding a total of six Super Bowl championships, tied for the most in league history.

While the Rooney Rule has made noteworthy but nominal progress in its impact on minority hiring in the National Football League, the spirit of the rule still lies within the organization of its namesake. A team that pioneered the scouting of historically Black colleges and universities and acquiring that talent to help build its Super Bowl dynasty of the 1970s and hired the NFL's first Black defensive coordinator (Dungy in 1984) has continued its reputation at the forefront of the league's efforts to integrate the upper levels of the game while still enjoying the success that has made it one of the game's most successful on the field.

23

TONY DUNGY

"MAKE THE SITUATION BETTER"

By Josh Taylor

O f the thirty-five NFL head coaches who have won a Super Bowl championship, only three won a Super Bowl previously as a player: Mike Ditka, Tom Flores and Tony Dungy. Of the three, Flores became the first Hispanic American coach to lift the Vince Lombardi Trophy when his Oakland Raiders beat the Philadelphia Eagles in Super Bowl XV. Dungy led the Indianapolis Colts to a victory over his protégé, Lovie Smith, and the Chicago Bears, in Super Bowl XLI. Dungy and Smith were the first two African American head coaches to reach the game, and Dungy was the first to win it.

Dungy's path to coaching in the NFL was an unlikely one, as has been described by Dungy himself. Following that path led to making history not only as a head coach but also as the first Black defensive coordinator in league history. But the course might be better charted with an understanding of Dungy's background, solidified by a remarkable family legacy and a series of experiences that would prepare him for such a legendary journey from his origins in Jackson, Michigan, to having his bust displayed in Canton, Ohio, in the Pro Football Hall of Fame.

Anthony Kevin Dungy was the son of two teachers. His mother, Cleomae, taught English at the local high school, and his father, Wilbur, was the chairman of the biology department at Jackson College. Wilbur earned his doctorate degree from Michigan State University, becoming one of the first Black PhDs in the state of Michigan, and then taught as a professor for

Tony Dungy, who became the first African American coordinator in the NFL with the Steelers, is shown during his days at the University of Minnesota, where he was a quarterback. *Courtesy of the University of Minnesota Athletics.*

more than twenty years at Delta College. Despite this being an accomplishment in the 1950s, Tony says his father very seldom spoke about it.

"Anytime he introduced himself, 'I'm Wil Dungy.' That's what he would say," Tony said in a long-form interview with longtime sportscaster James Brown called "Beyond the Game." "To me it was [a great accomplishment], but to him, that wasn't something that you talked about."

Before his stellar academic achievements, Wilbur Dungy served in the U.S. Army Air Force during World War II. What many people who know him did not know was that he flew as a pilot with the Tuskegee Airmen, the legendary 332nd Fighter Group made up of primarily Black fighter pilots. It was a revelation that his children were not aware of until the day of his funeral.

"A lot of people had memories of my dad, and one of his buddies got up and talked about my dad's life and talked about him being a Tuskegee Airman," Dungy said of his father's memorial. "All of us—kids, grandkids, everybody—were all floored. I never knew that. My dad would only say, 'Well, it was a time they didn't really want us to fly, so we had to teach ourselves.' That's all he ever said. I'd never put two and two together."

Dungy took that knowledge of his father as a lesson of both resilience and humility, two things that followed him throughout his life in football. The first example of that lesson came when Dungy was the starting quarterback at Parkside High School. Before his senior season, Dungy was named one of the team's captains, but his best friend, another standout player who was also African American, wasn't chosen. The Black players on the team suspected school officials would not allow two Black captains on the team, and they all quit in protest.

"I remember asking my dad about it: 'What do you think I should do?'" Dungy said. "And in his typical fashion, he said, 'We fought in World War II to give people the freedom, and to make America free so you get to make

Shown here is the 1975 University of Minnesota football team. In the third row, third from the end on the right, is Tony Dungy (9). Dungy led the team to a 6-5 mark, completing 54.7 percent of his passes for 1,515 yards and 15 touchdowns. *Courtesy of the University of Minnesota Athletics.*

that decision. But make your decision, not based on what everybody else is doing, what your friends are doing. What do you think is going to make the situation better?'"

Dungy ultimately decided the best way to make the situation better was to play, and he rejoined the team before his senior season began. A two-sport standout in both football and basketball, Dungy accepted an athletic scholarship to play football at the University of Minnesota. As the Golden

Gophers' starting quarterback, Dungy was named the team's most valuable player in 1975 and 1976 and was awarded the Big Ten Medal of Honor for athletic and academic excellence in 1977.

Despite his success as a quarterback in college, Dungy went unselected in the 1977 NFL draft. He was eventually signed by the Pittsburgh Steelers for a $2,000 signing bonus. Dungy eventually made the team under Hall of Fame head coach Chuck Noll, but as was customary with Black quarterbacks at the time, he changed positions, moving to the defensive side of the ball as a safety. During his rookie season, Dungy was called into action as the Steelers' emergency quarterback after starter Terry Bradshaw and backup Mike Kruczek were injured during an October 9 game against the Houston Oilers. During that game, Dungy intercepted a pass on defense and also threw an interception, becoming the most recent NFL player to do so.

Dungy's most notable season came in 1978, when he led the Steelers with 6 interceptions despite starting in only two of the team's sixteen games. That season, the Steelers' defense, led by the three remaining members of the famous "Steel Curtain" defensive line—Joe Greene, L.C. Greenwood and Dwight White—led the NFL with the fewest points allowed, and the Steelers went on to a 14-2 record and their third of four Super Bowl titles in six years.

After playing one final NFL season with the San Francisco 49ers the following year, by 1980, Dungy's playing days had come to an end, and he was hired by his alma mater, the University of Minnesota, as a defensive backs coach. Soon, Dungy's old head coach called with an opportunity to return to Pittsburgh and coach the defensive backs—some of them his old teammates—with the Steelers. Dungy coached the secondary for three seasons before eventually being promoted to defensive coordinator, becoming the league's first Black coordinator and its youngest ever at twenty-eight years old, after a conversation with Noll that Dungy recalled in his autobiography, *Quiet Strength*.

> *"Coach, have you given any thought to what you're going to do with the defensive coordinator position?"*
>
> *He looked startled. "Of course, Tony. Nobody knows as much about our defense as you do. That's always been my thought process since Woody left. You're our defensive coordinator."*
>
> *I blew out a breath and gave a rueful laugh, a mixture of relief and exasperation evident on my face. "Were you ever going to tell me that?"*
>
> *"Tony, you're our defensive coordinator."*
>
> *That was just the way Chuck was. Like when I went in at quarterback in 1977—I was the next man in line, even though I didn't know it. Things just kept moving along as planned—at least in his mind.*

In the first season with Dungy leading the Steelers defense, the team reached the AFC Championship Game, losing to second-year quarterback Dan Marino and the Miami Dolphins. But in the four seasons that followed, the eventual aging of that unit began to show, and the team got progressively worse, missing the playoffs all four years. Dungy recalls the end of his tenure after the 1988 season in *Quiet Strength*:

Both Donnie Shell and John Stallworth retired, and Mike Merriweather, the player we had counted on to be the cornerstone of our defense, became embroiled in a contract dispute and sat out the entire season. That was a big loss that we hadn't anticipated, especially in light of the fact that we had let some other veteran leaders go to allow for the development of the 1987 draft class.

Chuck was under a lot of heat and asked me to step down as coordinator, but to stay on staff as the defensive backs coach. I told him I would rather move on, so I resigned and started looking for a job. We were a long way from 1982, when Chuck had told a Pittsburgh paper that my coaching future was unlimited, that "[Tony could] go as far as he wants." Now I was going much farther than I wanted out of town.

Dungy's departure from Pittsburgh led to two more stops as an assistant coach: with the Kansas City Chiefs as Marty Schottenheimer's defensive backs coach (1989–91) and with the Minnesota Vikings as Dennis Green's defensive coordinator (1992–95). After fifteen years as an assistant, Dungy was hired by the Tampa Bay Buccaneers as their head coach before the 1996 season. Dungy was fired following six seasons in Tampa and then was hired by the Indianapolis Colts in 2002. He led them to a world championship during the 2006 season.

From unlikely professional player to history-making coach, Tony Dungy's time in the NFL is noted as one of the league's great underdog stories, a trailblazing journey that eventually led to football immortality.

24

GOING DIFFERENT DIRECTIONS

WASHINGTON & JEFFERSON'S WALTER COOPER AND DAN TOWLER

By David Finoli

After two unsuccessful seasons in 1942 and 1945 (the 1943 and 1944 seasons were canceled due to World War II), head coach–athletic director Pete Henry stepped aside as Washington & Jefferson's football coach, turning over the reins in 1946 to a man who had success as a high school coach, Henry Luecht. He immediately recruited two highly rated local African American players from the area who would become the major pieces in his backfield, Dan Towler and Walter Cooper. Towler was the more prominent recruit, leading Donora to successive Western Pennsylvania Interscholastic Athletic League (WPIAL) championships in 1944 and 1945. He had also run the 100-yard dash in under ten seconds, a rarity for the period. He was a 220-pound powerful runner and was considered an impressive acquisition by the school.

Cooper was also an impressive, speedy runner. He originally committed to play at Duquesne University. He explained in an interview with Rochester University that someone at Duquesne told him:

"Well, the University has scheduled Wake Forest and North Carolina State, Clemson and other schools in the south, and if we have an athlete of color on our squad, they will cancel the game." So I said, well, I said, "You mean to tell me that you would accept me full time as a student, but then deny me the opportunity to participate in all the extra-curricular activities which the institution offers." He said, "Well I don't make the rules." And I said—here

I am sixteen or seventeen years old—I said, "Well, I kinda understand that, but, under the circumstances, I cannot attend your institution."

Without a school to go to, he was contacted by a friend, one who had already committed to W&J.

So I had a friend whom I had competed against, in the Monongahela Valley in athletics by the name of Daniel Towler from Donora, Pennsylvania, who already had committed himself to go to Washington and Jefferson College in Washington, Pennsylvania. So he contacted me and he said, "Coop, where're you goin' to school?" And I said, "Well at this point in time I haven't— I'm out of it, and I'm left with the unenviable option of going to the services, becoming an eighteen-month GI, and then going to college on a GI bill." And he said, "Oh no, you ought to consider Washington and Jefferson College. I have a good contact there." So I went to Washington and Jefferson College, on an academic football scholarship.

Getting Cooper, who was an All–Monongahela Valley from Clairton, Pennsylvania, gave Luecht one of the fastest backfields in the country. They finished with a much-improved 6-2 mark in 1946, as Towler proved to be as good as advertised. He not only broke the school 100-yard dash record with a 9.9 mark in the spring but also was one of the leading scorers in the East. In the book *Battling the Indians, Panthers and Nittany Lions* by E. Lee North, which is a history of W&J football, North quoted a magazine called *She Produces All-Americans*, "Dan Towler, now in his second year of collegiate football, will blossom into one of the greatest of all time." The magazine compared him to the legendary Jim Thorpe, Red Grange and Eddie Mahan. It also said that Cooper was a fast addition that would also be a great complement in the backfield, but he was only a complement to Towler and not at his talent level, despite the fact he had scored 10 touchdowns both in 1947 and 1948 and was a star on the track team.

The team had average but disappointing seasons in Towler and Cooper's sophomore and junior years, finishing 4-5 and 5-3, respectively, despite the outstanding backfield. Towler had been a star in 1948, leading the nation in scoring with 133 points. The team had a dominant backfield by the two players' senior campaigns, nicknamed the "Four Gazelles" along with fullback Jack Sourbeer and quarterback Jimmy Hughes. While much was expected from the quartet, injuries and an unimaginative game plan saw the Presidents' record fall to 2-6.

The sports editor of the school newspaper, *The Red and Black*, Ken Abrams, said: "The offense was usually Towler through the line on first down, Towler off guard or tackle on second, then a pass or Cooper end run on third if a first down was not made. The trouble with such an offense is that if we in the press box knew it, certainly the opposing scouts and teams knew it."

Thus the careers of Towler and Cooper, while successful statistically, did not produce the wins most people expected. Dan Towler, who was a two-time All-American for the Presidents, went on to an outstanding NFL career, which prompted a 2020 article by *Sports Illustrated* claiming him to be the greatest running back nobody knew. He was third in the league in rushing in 1951 with 854 yards and a 6.78 per carry average, scoring the winning touchdown in the 1951 NFL championship to give the Los Angeles Rams the crown. He was a First-Team All-Pro in 1952, when he led the league in rushing, and was Second-Team in 1951, 1953 and 1954. He also was chosen to play in four Pro Bowls, being named the game's MVP in 1952, and he led the league in scoring during the 1952 and 1954 campaigns. By the time his career was done, he amassed 5,506 total yards, which was a Rams team record for years. Even though he graduated cum laude from W&J and had an outstanding pro career, when it came to achievements in integration outside the gridiron, it was Walker Cooper who stood ahead of the field.

Cooper was enamored with science, "because I didn't know any blacks who were scientists. I knew doctors, I knew pharmacists, I knew lawyers who were out of work, and I, and also knew dentists. But—so I took it as a challenge." He went on to become the first African American to receive a PhD in physical chemistry from the University of Rochester and went on to work for Eastman Kodak, where he received three patents for photographic film chemistry.

The Clairton native had a long career with Kodak, retiring in 1986, but he ended up with a legacy in fighting social injustice that is even more impressive. According to an article on the school's website, he had the following achievements:

- Founder, Action for a Better Community in Rochester, 1964
- Cofounded the National Urban League's Rochester chapter, 1965
- President of the NAACP Rochester Branch
- Elected to Board of Regents, New York State Education Department

- Established Rochester's Sister City program with Bamako, Mali, 1975; named a Knight of the National Order of Mali, 1981
- Received W&J's Distinguished Alumni Award, 1968; awarded honorary doctoral degree from W&J, 1987
- Elected to W&J's board of trustees, 1975; named a trustee emeritus, 2000
- Awarded honorary Doctor of Humane Letters by SUNY Geneseo, 2005
- Awarded Frederick Douglass Medal from the University of Rochester for his lifelong involvement in civil rights, 2008
- Rochester City School #10 is renamed the Dr. Walter Cooper Academy School #10, 2010

W&J even renamed a residence hall on campus after him in 2020. Dr. Cooper said at the dedication ceremony: "I just want to say that my life was shaped, my life was enriched, and my life led to dedication of other human beings based upon my early experience at Washington & Jefferson College. This is an honor that I will cherish forever, and I will pass it on to my children and hopefully my grandchildren, and generations of Coopers afterward."

In the end, Towler and Cooper represented themselves and the college proudly in their respective careers and were both elected to the school's Hall of Fame, Towler in 1999 and Cooper a year later. They were two stars going in different directions after graduation, but both had an enduring impact on the school.

IV
BOXING

25

FROM INTEGRATION TO WORLD TRAVEL TO ETERNAL CHAMPION

JACKIE WILSON

By Gary Kinn

Not much is known about "Pittsburgh" Jackie Wilson's birth and youth, nor about his professional boxing career, other than by historians of boxing or Pittsburgh history. That career and life is one that many people could only wish they had been lucky enough to experience.

Wilson was apparently born in Westminster, South Carolina, in 1909. Similar to the continued migration patterns in much of the United States during the first few years of the twentieth century, Wilson's family lived in Arkansas before their ultimate relocation to the Steel City, according to premier Pittsburgh boxing historian Roy McHugh. At some point during his youth, Wilson got involved in amateur boxing programs in the city. Pittsburgh was a major boxing center from 1900 to 1950, with all-time greats such as Harry Greb, Billy Conn and Fritzie Zivic active and well known in the sport both locally and nationally.

Professional boxing was an integrated sport well before other major sports in America. George Dixon of Halifax, Nova Scotia, was the first Black fighter to win a world title, at bantamweight in 1892, and he was named the greatest featherweight of all time by no less of an authority than Nat Fleisher, the founder of *Ring Magazine*, "the Bible of Boxing."

Jackie Wilson fought the majority of his career between the flyweight limit of 112 to 115 pounds and the lightweight limit of 135 pounds, with the majority of his bouts taking place at the featherweight limit of 126

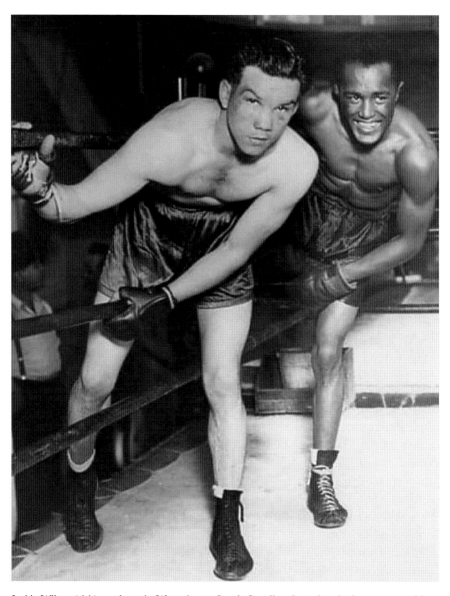

Jackie Wilson (*right*) was born in Westminster, South Carolina, but when he became a world-renowned boxer, he called Pittsburgh home. The highlight of Wilson's career took place on November 18, 1941, when he defeated Richie Lemos in Los Angeles to capture the National Boxing Association's World Featherweight championship. Wilson is pictured here with his stable mate, Jackie Carter. *Courtesy of Douglas Cavanaugh.*

pounds. No less of an expert than Johnny Ray noticed the talented Wilson in amateur fights around Pittsburgh and introduced him to his original managers in order to turn professional. Ray's eye for talent was a qualified opinion; he was a former pro featherweight fighter himself from 1913 to 1924 and later became more distinguished as both the manager and cornerman for the great light heavyweight Conn.

Two months after the stock market crash and the beginning of the Great Depression, Wilson made his professional debut on December 6, 1929, at a Moose Lodge in Pittsburgh. Wilson weighed in at 115 pounds and won his first pro bout over six rounds by unanimous decision. Wilson would win many fights in similar fashion throughout his career, as he was a pure boxer, rather than an all-attacking fighter who relied primarily on power punches or damaging blows to win. Similar in boxing style to a modern-era Pernell Whitaker or Paul Spadafora, Wilson was a fast-handed, lighter hitting fighter who lived and succeeded by the "hit and not get hit" philosophy, which undoubtedly allowed him to continue to fight and record over 150 bouts over the subsequent seventeen years. Jackie was technically sound, elusive and well-conditioned, and he could throw combinations in bunches, no matter the contracted fight distance. One Pittsburgh trainer stated that "the only time you'll touch Jackie, is when you touch gloves before the fight."

Wilson started his professional career with 4 wins and 1 draw. In Jackie's sixth pro fight, he was matched with another Pittsburgh-based prospect, Mose Butch. Butch was also a very good amateur prospect in the city, and he had won national amateur championships prior to his pro start against Wilson. Butch was a more rugged fighter than Wilson, but the two young prospects battled to a six-round draw at the Motor Square Garden in the city. Butch and Wilson would get to know each other well over the next four years, with five fights occurring between the two men. Butch would actually win over Jackie after his debut in two of their next three fights, placing Jackie at an early uncertain career position of 4-3-2 after his first nine pro bouts.

After the second loss to Butch in September 1930, Wilson began a hot streak that saw him win 13 of his next 15 fights. Every fight was contested in the Pittsburgh area, and Jackie performed at such famed boxing venues as Duquesne Gardens, the Northside Arena and Greenlee Field, in addition to Motor Square and Hickey Park Bowl in Millvale. Hickey Park was an outdoor and intimate arena accessible via trolley. On Monday nights in the summer, steelworkers could leave their shifts and stop in the Brown Jug tavern on-site before watching pro boxing at high levels. In 1932, Wilson's talent and potential were becoming recognized enough in the Pittsburgh area that he was matched with respected veteran Wee Willie Davies in February 1932 at Kapphan's Arena in the city. The bout was contracted at 122 pounds at what would now be called a junior featherweight limit. The veteran Davies came into the match at an astounding 122 wins, 20 losses and 17 draws, and Wilson proved his matchmakers right when he won the major test by unanimous decision over ten rounds. The bout also put fight fans on notice.

Continuing his rise, Wilson went another 7 wins and 2 losses before being matched with Midget Wolgast of Philadelphia in February 1933. Wolgast had battled in a significant portion of his career as a flyweight or bantamweight, or a limit of 112 to 122 pounds, and he had accumulated 121 wins in his career coming into the bout. Wolgast is considered one of the fastest flyweights in history, but he was often somewhat undisciplined in training and reportedly also had regular trouble staying near contracted fighting weights. Wilson had also lost to Ross Fields by a knockout for one of the few times in his career in his bout just prior to the scheduled Wolgast contest, and that may have been a factor in Wolgast agreeing to fight. Perhaps the strains of making weight for both men, or Wolgast's similar speed, combined to give Wilson the fits that he was used to giving his foes. The anticipated bout and result were both disappointments to many ringside observers. Although the bout was officially ruled a controversial draw, most who witnessed it felt Wolgast won the scrap, with the hometown *Pittsburgh Press* giving Jackie only two or three rounds of the ten in which he was the better man. Despite the unsatisfactory result, a telling factor regarding the difficulty of fighting Wilson could potentially be found in the fact that no rematch occurred between the two men.

Undeterred, Wilson agreed to a match with Tommy Paul only sixty days after the Wolgast draw back at the Motor Square Garden. Paul was known for his come-forward and, at times, mauling style. The Buffalo, New York native had also beaten many good Pittsburgh fighters, similar to what Wolgast had done as an outsider who came to the city. Paul was placed at as much as a 10-1 favorite over Wilson prior to the match, and some press even referred to Jackie as a potential sacrifice. But as one of the things that will always be an appeal of the sweet science, Wilson out-boxed the punishing Paul over ten rounds in a somewhat disputed decision. In a rematch arranged just sixty days later back at Hickey Park, Wilson won even more decisively, reopening a cut over Paul's eye that he had caused in the first fight and winning via TKO stoppage after the eighth round.

The take-notice, dual wins over Paul set Wilson on the best and most interesting trajectory of both his fighting career and his life. Spurred by the wins over Paul, Wilson set out on another streak of 10 wins, 2 losses and 1 draw before taking on Sammy Angott of Washington, Pennsylvania, in July 1935, again at his second home, Hickey Park. Although the fight was early in his career, Angott's rough, mauling and downright clutching style was a problem for any opponent and ultimately led to his place among the best fighters in Pittsburgh ring history. Jackie won a unanimous six-round decision to continue his path. After that victory, Wilson would rip off a stunning 21 wins in his next 23 fights over a two-year period with the intention to get himself back into contention for a major title. It was where Wilson did the majority of the work that was so unusual.

One of the perverse aspects of pro boxing is that very good fighters such as Wilson are often avoided by matchmakers due to the risk of their fighter losing to them. And this results in the potential for subsequent lower paydays due to the loss. In addition, boxers who rely on speed and skill similar to Jackie are also often the most avoided class, posing the highest risk to opponents of getting embarrassed by their skill and technique. Due to these factors, and the fact that Jackie had to continue to build a big winning streak to get more national consideration, his managers sent him to England, Ireland and Scotland for the majority of 1936. And he complied, winning 11 of 12 bouts there before returning to Pittsburgh. The precedent for African American fighters traveling to Europe and Australia for both marketing and financial reasons had been set by turn-of-the-century fighters such as Sam McVey, Joe Jeannette, Sam Langford and even Jack Johnson.

The business strategy for Wilson seemed to work, as he ripped off another 9 wins in 10 bouts when he returned to the States. Shortly after his return, he was matched with Speedy Dado across the country in Stockton, California, in July 1937. Dado had over 102 wins coming in, and the two fighters' ring styles were similar, which had many fans looking forward to the scrap. Wilson won fairly easily on points, and this made him a recognized commodity on the boxing-mad West Coast. It would turn out to be a fruitful and important victory with a likely effect on Wilson's future career.

On the return to Pittsburgh, Wilson ran into a fairly large bump in the title road. He fought to 3 draws with the respected Leo Rodak of Chicago and suffered a loss to Angott, this time in Milwaukee. The draws and setbacks resulted in a fairly inactive year in 1938. Similar to before, Jackie and his managers again set off for another world sojourn, this time to Australia in February 1939. In the seven months until August 1939, fighting in the exotic locales of Brisbane, Sydney and Melbourne, he won a staggering 13 straight fights. The previous tactic seemed to work better this time, as Wilson began boxing in many other cities in America on his return, including Baltimore, Chicago, New Orleans and Cincinnati. He fought and lost a close unanimous decision to all-time great featherweight Chalky Wright in Baltimore. Wilson's renewed reputation and willingness to go anywhere finally, and ultimately, led to the crowning moment of his professional career.

In November 1941, Wilson was matched with Richie Lemos of Southern California for the National Boxing Association (NBA) featherweight title at the Olympic Auditorium in Los Angeles. The NBA was the forerunner of what is now the World Boxing Association (WBA), and the significance of this title and championship cannot be ignored. The WBA remains to this day one of the four current major sanctioning bodies with major influence and important management responsibility for the sport. In addition, the NBA was likely the first organization in the professional sport to attempt to implement standard and universal rules, establish safety standards to protect combatants in the ring and focus on reducing corruption. Jackie was unusually coming off 3 straight losses (the loss to Wright and 2 to nemesis Rodak again) prior to the NBA scheduled title bout. That may have been a big reason why Lemos signed the fight contract.

Under the bright lights of the famed Olympic Auditorium, Wilson reached the pinnacle of his career by defeating Lemos on points over twelve rounds to win the NBA title. And he did so again just nine days after Pearl Harbor and just four weeks after the first fight between the two skilled technicians. Both fights followed the same pattern, with Jackie building up early points leads on judges' scorecards and withstanding aggression from Lemos late in the fights to win by decision. Wilson's name would be forever listed in boxing annals as a world champion after eleven long years and after all of the punishment accumulated from training and more than 100 fights to date.

Sadly, winning the title didn't propel Wilson to greater success. He didn't defend his title or fight often during 1942. He also suffered 2 straight nontitle losses, one due to a criticized decision in Boston, and he suffered a major forearm injury in the other loss in New York City. The effects of inactivity and injury after the championship defeats of Lemos likely led to consecutive fifteen-round decision losses to New England's Jackie Callura in 1943, in which he relinquished his NBA title. Wilson never regained the title, but he was still marketable and respected enough to be matched with great Willie Pep at Duquesne Gardens in 1943. In his last fight in the long career on Pittsburgh soil, Jackie dropped a competitive decision over twelve heats to the great Pep at the famous venue. He would drop another decision to Pep in Kansas City in 1946.

A common saying in pro boxing is that most careers don't end in a pretty fashion. Jackie Wilson's career did not, losing as much as he won across the country and before finally reaching the West Coast for a second time. In California, Canada and Mexico, Wilson was able to find a multitude of smaller fighters to box, with opponents largely interested in building a reputation on his name. He lost eleven of his final thirteen bouts in Los Angeles, Oakland, San Jose, San Francisco, Spokane, Vancouver, British Columbia and one at a bullfighting ring in Juarez, Mexico.

Despite the ending to this amazing story, integration and migration to Pittsburgh gave Jackie Wilson a life that few others will experience. He became a fan favorite in a tough-minded, hard-judgement sports town, a great accomplishment during the tight-money years and hardships of the Great Depression. He defeated numerous opponents who either were, or became, world champions. He became one himself after years of competition and did so in the fabled, historic Olympic Auditorium in Los Angeles. Wilson performed throughout the United States, from coast to coast, at a time when many couldn't hope to travel to or even physically see such places. He visited, saw and lived on two other continents thanks to his boxing career. Jackie had his hand raised exactly one hundred times in victory in his chosen profession, with many of those coming before fans in his adopted hometown. He was posthumously named to the World Boxing Hall of Fame. Wilson will always hold and have successfully defended the NBA/WBA Featherweight Title in the annals of the sport. Here's a toast somewhere in Millvale or Pittsburgh to you, Featherweight Boxing Champion of the World "Pittsburgh" Jackie Wilson.

26

A FAIR CHANCE NO EXCEPTIONS

INTEGRATING PITTSBURGH BOXING

By Douglas Cavanaugh

African American prizefighters found a home in Pittsburgh in a way that couldn't be matched in other major cities across the United States in the early to mid-twentieth century. Most of the Black boxers back then agreed that the Smoky City gave them an opportunity to get a fair shake in the business, mostly because the infamous "color line" was not recognized or allowed here. Promoters Red Mason and Jules Beck were adamant that if you wanted to fight in Pittsburgh, you had to fight and beat the best men around, which more often than not meant facing our "ebony-hued" brethren in the ring, many of whom were firmly ensconced at the top of the ratings in several divisions.

This meant that fighters like John Henry Lewis and Jackie Wilson were able to realize their championship dreams as Pittsburgh residents and Charley Burley and Harry Bobo at least came within sniffing distance but fell just short for various reasons. Sugar Ray Robinson, Joe Louis, Ezzard Charles, Archie Moore and Henry Armstrong all came here before they became world champions in order to cash in on the lively fight scene, Robinson and Charles finding it especially lucrative and Armstrong and Moore finding the fistic landscape to be a bit more difficult to navigate. (Louis fought here just once, winning by knockout. He afterward mostly stuck to the larger cities for the remainder of his career.)

But predating all of those glorious names were the pioneer African Americans of the sport, many of whom graced Pittsburgh rings just after the turn of the century. Joe Walcott, the first Black welterweight world champion, fought here, as did Jack Johnson. Johnson had his second fight as heavyweight champion at Duquesne Gardens when he took on local favorite Tony Ross the day Forbes Field opened. Johnson, who had been recently criticized for picking on smaller opposition and fighting conservatively, threw caution to the wind and aggressively pounded the larger Ross, flooring and bloodying the brave Italian in giving one of the most scintillating performances of his career.

Many great uncrowned African Americans fought here as well, such as lightweight/welterweight legend Jack Blackburn (later to become famous as Joe Louis's trainer) and smooth-boxing heavyweight contender Joe Jeannette. Sam Langford, the greatest nonchampion of them all and inarguably the most avoided fighter in history, contested twice in Pittsburgh to great acclaim. When Sam fought Mike Schreck on November 23, 1909, at Old City Hall, Jack Johnson was in town doing a play.

Though he had been the champion for less than a year, Johnson was already procuring a reputation as a fighter who wanted to avoid risk, which meant not giving his leading contenders a deserved chance at his crown. Langford, a terrible puncher, was Johnson's top challenger for the title at this time and was feeling rightfully snubbed by Jack, who had just given middleweight champion Stanley Ketchel an undeserved title fight.

Under these circumstances, and being in the same city at the same time, meant that it wouldn't take long before the two engaged in a war of words in the local press. Langford began hurling challenges, and Johnson deftly dismissed and evaded them, all the while teasing Sam (and the fight crowd) with promises of a bout if Langford put up the required money.

The tension got so bad that it almost ended in gunplay, or seemingly so. According to Langford's manager, Joe Woodman, Sam was at a club on Wylie Avenue in the Hill District with his friend Bob Armstrong, who was Johnson's sparring partner. Johnson suddenly appeared with his manager, George Little, in tow, looking for Armstrong. The champ was incensed to find Bob together with Sam and began to berate him, even going so far as insisting that Armstrong leave the club immediately.

After listening to Johnson lay into his pal for a bit, Langford stepped in and let Jack know that it was he who wasn't welcome at the club and that he and Little had better leave. According to Woodman (and later corroborated by the man who broke it up and disarmed Johnson and Little), Jack and his manager both grabbed at their hip pockets. A detective who happened to be there quickly wrestled what turned out to be an unloaded gun away from Johnson and a gun from Little.

"It's a good thing that gun is empty," he warned the champ. "If it was loaded I'd run you in so quick it'd make your hair stand on end."

Langford, angered that Johnson would pull a firearm on him, suggested that they slug it out right then and there. Johnson dismissed the idea, going quickly from threats of gunplay to suddenly taking on the airs of a gentleman prizefighter who, as "champion of the world," couldn't allow himself to sink so low as to engage in a lowly nightclub brawl. The airs put on by Johnson, as well as the false professional ethics he was espousing that he had contradicted by pulling a gun moments earlier, obviously enraged Langford, and it was hard for those present to keep the "Boston Terror" from attacking the "Galveston Giant."

According to the detective who broke up the altercation, the numerous nightclub patrons were apparently sympathetic to Langford and were possibly on the verge of taking up his cause when Johnson and company made their hasty exit from the premises.

In many ways, it turned out to be something of a microcosm of the story of the rest of Johnson's boxing career. The crowds continued to despise him and his arrogant, dismissive ways (among other reasons), and Jack kept avoiding and ducking the very worthy challenges of his number one challenger, Sam Langford. Not only was it unacceptable in this city but also in the sporting world at large.

Just another wild story in the history of boxing in Pittsburgh, where, whether Black or white, you either took on the best fighters or were quickly shown the door. No exceptions.

27

HARRY BOBO

By Douglas Cavanaugh

Hill District hotshot Harry Bobo was an imposing figure during a heavyweight era full of imposing figures. One of the top contenders for Joe Louis's title in the 1940s, Bobo had it all: size, strength, power and athletic ability. He also possessed a powerful punch and scored 24 knockouts in his 35 wins. He was called the "Peabody Paralyzer," a tip of the hat from his days as a star athlete at Peabody High School, where he was a football hero and a track-and-field standout. His athletic exploits there were a source of pride for the entire city of Pittsburgh, and he was often covered in the newspapers. But it was in the fight game that he earned his greatest acclaim.

Harry stood six feet, four inches tall and weighed 210 pounds, a big heavyweight for that era. Pittsburgh sports impresario Barney McGinley regarded him as the greatest prospect he ever saw, and even former heavyweight champion Jack Johnson was impressed enough to drop by the gym to dispense some advice to the promising young pugilist. From his pro debut on, Bobo's career was closely followed by local sportswriters. He was eventually regarded highly enough to be considered "duration champion" by Ohio and Maryland while de facto champion Joe Louis was in the army and his title was "frozen" during World War II.

Cleveland heavyweight Lem Franklin was a murderous puncher as well and was considered by many to have an even harder punch than Joe Louis. In fact, he and Bobo were considered two of the biggest bangers in the division in the 1940s. As such, the boxing public couldn't wait to see these two boys matched, and the Rooney-McGinley Boxing Club made sure they got their wish on March 30, 1942.

Duquesne Gardens was sold out on that record-breaking night, and a reported five thousand people had to be turned away from the box office. At the sound of the bell, Franklin went right after Bobo in an attempt to end the night early with a blitzkrieg of leather. Before a single minute had elapsed, he floored the surprised Hill District boy with a crushing right hand. Bobo rose on unsteady legs and immediately began to backpedal so as to get his bearings and halt the rushes of his antagonist. Franklin charged in again, this time almost folding Bobo in half with two thunderous blows to the ribs during a clinch. Things were looking bad for the local favorite.

Sensing the kill, Lem pounced on his wounded prey but was wild with his punches. The "Peabody Paralyzer," who was thoroughly battered and outfought for the first two minutes of the fight, began to assert his strength and measure "Lammin' Lem" with his own powerful shots. The audience went crazy as the two giants took turns staggering each other, bulldozing uppercuts and slamming hooks on the inside. During one exchange, Bobo cut loose with a huge right cross, dumping Franklin on his back. Lem got up at the count of eight and attempted to backpedal, but Harry knew better than to let this dangerously wounded leopard off the hook. He quickly cornered his adversary and hooked a left and crossed with his right, dropping Franklin again.

The Clevelander barely beat the referee's count. He clambered to his feet, only to be met with another crushing right. Lem dropped as if he'd been deboned, his head draped over the bottom rope. He was out cold. It was a wildly entertaining (albeit brief) shootout, and both Barney McGinley and Pittsburgh Steelers head coach Walter Kiesling called it the most exciting fight they ever saw. Only the Solly Krieger–Oscar Rankins contest could make a claim to being the more entertaining battle.

Sadly, neither fighter would realize his dream of contesting with Joe Louis for the title. In 1944, Bobo was forced into retirement due to eye problems. Franklin died later the same year due to head injuries suffered in a bout he never should have taken.

But Harry stayed close to the fight game regardless, watching from ringside and occasionally refereeing bouts. He loved the game and obviously never forgot Jack Johnson's generosity to him during his youth, making it a point to help future contenders like Bob Baker to get started in their own careers. In later years, he became a preacher and a bartender before dying in 1966 at age forty-six. His former manager, Eddie Kapphan, believed his death was due to damage sustained from a sparring session years earlier with the murderous-hitting Curtis "Hatchetman" Sheppard, who was his stablemate. From that day on, Bobo often complained of headaches and was said to be complaining about them shortly before his untimely passing.

But Harry Bobo gave enough thrills and exciting fights during the 1940s to earn his place in Pittsburgh boxing's Valhalla.

28

JOHN HENRY LEWIS

CAREER REVIVED IN PITTSBURGH BY GUS GREENLEE

By Douglas Cavanaugh

African American boxers have always been prominent in Pittsburgh's fight history. For some reason the Steel City, while still a town of racial segregation back in the day, was much more liberal than most cities in its treatment of Black prizefighters. Red Mason, who pretty much ran the sport from the late 1800s until the 1920s, had a controlling interest in most boxers in Pittsburgh during his time, and he absolutely forbade his fighters to draw the "color line."

The blowback from the disastrous reign of heavyweight champion Jack Johnson was felt by Black prizefighters all over the country, and for years world titles that had long been available to them were now out of reach. But they flocked to the western Pennsylvania fight scene regardless, anxious to earn the dollars that could still be earned. By the mid- to late 1920s and early 1930s, things began to look up a bit as Black fighters once again began to fight for, and win, world titles. Fighters like Tiger Flowers, Young Jack Thompson and Panama Al Brown rose to the pinnacle of the sport and inspired many young "colored" boxers to dream bigger and aim higher.

Things really took an upswing when John Henry Lewis moved to Pittsburgh in the spring of 1935 and won the world light-heavyweight championship six months later. He became the centerpiece of a new stable of Black prizefighters under the guidance of Hill District kingpin Gus Greenlee, the first Black manager of a world champion boxer. A smooth boxer and sharp hitter, Lewis appealed to both the purists and the kayo-hungry, and Pittsburgh took great pride in his achievements despite him being a transplant.

Perhaps his most important achievement was realized when he fought Al Gainer on July 30, 1936, at Forbes Field. Gainer was an exciting and popular boxer who fought in Pittsburgh often. He was also a top contender for the light-heavyweight title. Never one to duck a challenge, Lewis and Greenlee decided to give Gainer a twelve-round, nontitle try. The highly anticipated bout was hyped as a "natural." It was the proverbial classic boxer versus puncher matchup, and the presale numbers were huge.

A happy bonus for sportswriters all over was the simmering feud building in the respective corners of both fighters. Former heavyweight champion Jack Johnson had taken an interest in Gainer and decided to train him for the fight. Perhaps not so coincidentally, Jack Blackburn, Johnson's age-old enemy (who had recently had him ejected from the Joe Louis camp for disparaging the future champion), took over "active charge" of Lewis's training duties shortly thereafter.

The verbal barbs soon began to fly, and the press ate up every word. Blackburn was no doubt still smarting from his prize pupil's loss to Max Schmeling weeks earlier—a loss that Johnson had loudly predicted to anyone who would listen. Johnson wasted no time in pouring salt into Blackburn's raw wound. "Louis will never see the day that he is as good a fighter as either Gainer or John Henry," Johnson crowed. "They are natural born fighters. Louis is a newspaper champion." Then getting down to the business at hand, Johnson warned that "John Henry Lewis had better be in perfect condition or take the worst licking since he bagged the championship."

Gainer, a soft-spoken type who was never inclined to boast or threaten, was apparently allowing Johnson to influence him, as was evidenced by his boldly predicting a knockout over the champion. Lewis (and Blackburn) responded in kind, cautioning Al (and Johnson) not to get too cocky. "If Gainer thinks he is going to stop me, he is sadly mistaken and is going to get the surprise of his life," John Henry warned.

After weeks of this sort of back and forth, the fight crowd was primed and ready for this bout, which would be the second largest in Pittsburgh boxing history at the time, just behind the Teddy Yarosz–Vince Dundee middleweight championship fight two years earlier. It was the absolute largest in the city for a nontitle bout, thus putting a crimp in the long-held belief in boxing that a match between two "colored" fighters doesn't draw at the box office.

The undercard featured three future Hall of Fame boxers working their way up through the undercard ranks. The first was future lightweight king Sammy Angott, fighting in his seventeenth pro bout and copping a six-round decision over Lawrenceville's Irish Billy Miller, who would go on to be a top lightweight contender in later years. The second bout featured teenaged Billy Conn, who was fighting his fourth bout against then-archrival Teddy Movan of McKeesport. Conn nipped a close eight-round decision. The third bout had future welterweight champion Fritzie Zivic chopping down Laddie Tonelli in the sixth round of a ten-rounder. Lewis's stablemate, Honeyboy Jones, was also on the card and made an impressive showing in stopping Bill Schwerin in seven rounds.

The undercard bouts were a smashing success across the board, so much so that when it was time for the main event, the crowd was at a fever pitch. Gainer came down the aisle first with a grinning Jack Johnson in tow. Moments later, champion Lewis made his appearance with a glowering Jack Blackburn by his side. The animosity between the jovial Johnson and the saturnine Blackburn couldn't have been more pronounced as they glared across the ring at each other. The time for talk and reckless braggadocio was over.

At the sound of the first bell, Gainer pounced on Lewis, jumping to an early lead and shading the first three rounds by pressing the champion and hooking hard to the body with his deadly left. Lewis began to come to life in the middle rounds, showcasing his boxing skills and dazzling footwork as he began to find the range with his vaunted jab. Gainer opened a cut on Lewis's right eye in the sixth, a favor which John Henry returned three rounds later when he split Gainer's right eye. The *Pittsburgh Post-Gazette* commented that the two were "on each other like a pair of Bengal tigers" as they stepped up the action.

The fight was either man's for the taking as they neared the end, but it was Lewis who stepped it up in the final stanzas, using his superior versatility and speed to outbox Gainer, who was briefly floored in the final seconds of the bout. Both men bled freely at the end, but it was the champion who took away the unanimous points verdict after a thrilling contest.

Over in the Gainer corner, Jack Johnson was done flashing his cocky smile as Lewis's hand was raised, while Blackburn no doubt wore a self-satisfied smirk over having finally gotten the better of Johnson after so many years of ill-feeling.

V
OTHER SPORTS

29

THE GREAT ESCAPE

THE STORY OF JOHN WOODRUFF'S 1936 GOLD MEDAL RUN

By David Finoli

The date was August 4, 1936, in Berlin, Germany, in front of Adolf Hitler and 110,000 fans at the Olympiastadion (Olympic Stadium). The event was the men's 800-meter final. John Woodruff looked to be struggling with the race almost halfway done. He had come here along with seventeen other African Americans set on embarrassing Hitler's philosophy of Aryan supremacy. The eighteen would eventually capture fourteen medals, which frustrated Hitler to the point that he would neither meet nor congratulate them on their accomplishments.

Woodruff had started with the philosophy that he would follow behind the leader, presumably the other Black runner in the field, Canada's Phil Edwards, who usually set out on a fast pace. He then wanted to burst at the end past him to capture the gold medal. At this point of the race, the strategy was failing. Edwards was going much slower than expected, and three other runners had come to Woodruff's right, effectively blocking him in and giving him few options to get past them.

Born in Connellsville, Woodruff attended high school as the nation was mired in the Great Depression. He started out playing football but had to quit the team because practice conflicted with his home chores. He dropped out of school at one point to try to secure a job in a glass factory, but it wasn't interested in hiring an African American, so he went back to school, where an assistant football coach remembered how fast he was and

Connellsville's John Woodruff not only became a star at the University of Pittsburgh in the 800-meter run but also captured a gold medal at the 1936 Berlin Olympic Games in one of the most exciting races in the history of the games. *Courtesy of the University of Pittsburgh Athletics.*

recruited him for the track team, promising that he would have him home in time to do his chores.

After failing at the shot put and discus, he was talked into utilizing his long stride and running in the half mile. It was a perfect fit—so perfect that with the help of some local businessmen, he secured a scholarship on the University of Pittsburgh track team, where he would be one of twelve Black students on a campus of over twelve thousand. Woodruff eventually finished second in the AAU (Amateur Athletic Union) championships in the

800-meter run, which qualified him for the Olympic trials. The freshman ended up winning the trials, falling only 0.1 seconds off the world record. All of a sudden, the little-known Pitt freshman was the favorite to win the gold medal at the Berlin Olympics.

While the Olympics were awarded to Berlin in 1931, two years before Hitler took power, they were now being held with a background of controversy. Aryan supremacy was being promoted, and the Nazi Party newspaper was pushing for a ban of Jewish and Black athletes. Because of this, some in Europe and the United States were calling for a boycott. That never came to fruition, and Woodruff would get the chance to make a stronger statement in the race.

It had been twenty-four years since an American had won a gold medal in the 800, but after a very impressive semifinal victory, it looked like that streak might come to an end—until Woodruff found himself in trouble 300 meters into the race. He was young and lacked experience in the big races, although perhaps it was his lack of experience that would serve him well now.

In an article in Azcentral.com, Woodruff claimed: "I was very inexperienced. Coming from a small town it was very overwhelming to me. Phil Edwards jumped right in front and set a very, very slow pace. I decided due to my lack of experience that I would follow him. The pace was so slow and all the runners crowded around me. I had enough experience to know if I tried to get out of the trap I was going to be disqualified."

It was here that his inexperience led him to try a bold move, perhaps the boldest in Olympic history. He pulled into the third lane and almost came to a halt (Woodruff claims he did stop) and let the runners get past him. It was almost as if he was starting the race a second time. His long strides were now on display, eventually leading him past all the runners going into the stretch. He lost the lead for a moment to Italy's Mario Lanzi before bolting past him and holding him off at the finish line to give him a dramatic gold medal.

Hitler was furious that another Black athlete had won a gold and refused to meet Woodruff. The Pitt freshman hardly noticed, saying: "The [German] people were very, very cordial. They just crowded around us and asked for autographs. It seemed like they were very anxious to be friendly."

The leaders of the Nazi Party were not anxious to be friendly; neither were many people back home, where America still was plagued with racial prejudice. Woodruff was left back at Pitt for a meet at the U.S. Naval Academy, because navy didn't want to compete against a Black athlete. He was reportedly robbed of a world record at the 1937 Pan-American Games when it was ruled that the track he ran on wasn't of an official distance, so the record didn't count. He was angry with the Pitt coach for the navy incident and tried to convince future Olympic bronze medalist Herb Douglas not to attend Pitt.

He admitted later on: "Certainly I was bitter about the way we were treated, but what could we do? If we stopped running who would we be hurting? Only ourselves. We just ran and did the best we could."

It was an attitude that would help other African American athletes to be accepted and achieve success in track and field. It all started with Woodruff's great escape on the Olympic track in Berlin, still arguably the most daring maneuver in Olympic track history.

30

THE LEGENDARY SPORTSWRITERS OF THE
PITTSBURGH COURIER

By Samuel W Black

From 1910 to the mid-1950s, *Pittsburgh Courier* sports coverage was dominated by boxing and baseball. Sportswriters and editors William Nunn Sr., Chester Washington, W. Rollo Wilson and Wendell Smith were the early pioneers of what would become one of the best sports sections of any Black weekly paper. During the first decade of the paper, boxing and baseball teams regularly appeared in the reporting. Not until the early 1920s did a true sports section develop under Bill Nunn Sr. The *Courier* had yet to develop its crusading focus on sports in these early years. When it did, the paper agitated for integration in these two major sports. By catering to the African American community and reporting on sports the community would be interested in, social and political issues such as integration, civil rights and economic fairness became major concerns. Andrew Buni mentioned that in 1927 the *Courier* didn't even report on Babe Ruth's 60 home runs but instead was exclusively focused on the playing of the Homestead Grays.

From 1900 to 1947, sports were largely segregated in America. Baseball and boxing were the exceptions. Although the color line did exist in Major League Baseball, the Homestead Grays found opportunities to play non-MLB white teams in exhibition games or sandlot contests. Boxing was a different story.

Prizefighting opened to Black pugilists primarily because of the gambling associated with it. From the very beginning, the sport was a gambling activity and not so much centered on an organized club, as

The Westinghouse High School basketball team included Bill Nunn (*second in the row from the left*) and Chuck Cooper (*standing to his right*). While Cooper went on to a Hall of Fame career with the Boston Celtics, Nunn became not only a tremendous writer with the *Pittsburgh Courier* but also a Hall of Fame scout with the Pittsburgh Steelers. *Courtesy of Duquesne University Athletics.*

the other major sports were. Champions like Joe Gans and Jack Johnson dominated white fighters on a regular basis. Other Black fighters such as Sam Langford, Joe Jeannette, Harry Wills and Sam McVey did not have an opportunity to fight for the title. Even champion Jack Johnson drew the color line in defending his title against fellow Black heavyweights. Racism has its peculiarities. Johnson didn't think a boxing public would pay much to see two Black fighters duking it out for the world's heavyweight title. Maybe he was right. McVey, Jeannette, Langford and Wills never had a chance at the title Johnson held. Once Johnson lost the title in 1915, white fighters again drew the color line, and it would be twenty-three years before another African American would fight for the heavyweight championship. Integration in the ring appeared mostly in the lower weight classes. Welterweight champion Joe Walcott, lightweight champion Joe Gans and featherweight champion George Dixon regularly fought white opponents in title bouts and preliminaries. In his 1933 *Courier* column Sports Spurts, Rollo Wilson devised a top-ten greatest fighter list regardless of race, and seven of the ten were African Americans.

Baseball and boxing received crusading coverage from the *Courier*. Two major events that impacted the history of sports in America were championed by the *Courier*: baseball's integration and in boxing the rise of Joe Louis as heavyweight king. Both concerns were national and local news. By the 1920s, the *Courier*'s sportswriters and columnists had developed their own expertise. Nunn and Wilson were experts in numerous sports, while Washington focused on boxing. When Wendell Smith joined the paper in 1938, a true baseball journalist was on the team. Smith was not a run-of-the-mill sports journalist but one with the aptitude to challenge the color line both in the press box and on the field. Both Nunn Sr. and Washington had addressed the integration of MLB before Smith joined the paper. The paper had the headline "New York Daily Says Big Leagues Should Drop the Color Line," with a byline article, "Colorful Stars Would Stimulate Interest in National Past Time" from the *Daily*'s editorial. The players mentioned as possible MLB players were Ted Page, outfielder for the Pittsburgh Crawfords; Willie Wells, shortstop for the St. Louis Stars; and Larry Brown, catcher for the New York Black Yankees. The paper would continue to agitate for integration in subsequent issues, suggesting Negro league players who would "add color" to the big leagues. *Courier* sports editor Chester Washington set up the "Big League Symposium" in his Sez Ches column to solicit further MLB comment on Negro players in the majors. Washington did an article about longtime Pirates assistant trainer George Asten, an African American who joined the club in 1909. He was held up by Pirates ownership as their example of racial tolerance. In his 1938 piece on Asten, Washington saluted him, saying, "trainer extraordinary [*sic*], accepted by the Pirates, a credit to the game and his race."

Wendell Smith would escalate the issue with continued journalistic discussion on integration. His campaign progressed from 1938 to 1947. Smith saved most of his criticism for major league owners, who "always dodge and neglect" the color question. He suggested African American baseball fans form an organization to fight Major League Baseball over the color issue. His belief was that the fight for integration of the major leagues should take on a civil rights persona with an organization the likes of the NAACP. An organizational approach would remove the individual campaign and replace it with a collective campaign. This strategy was the cornerstone of Smith's effort to integrate baseball. In all, it was a ten-year campaign for Smith leading up to Jackie Robinson's signing.

Following Smith's 1938 lead, the New York Trade Union, one of the largest union umbrellas of the AFL-CIO, at its second annual convention decided to attach the "Ending Jim Crowism in Baseball" day to its convention lineup during the New York World's Fair of 1940.

With organized labor pushing the envelope, Smith's campaign was picking up momentum beyond the sport and into labor. Smith wanted to tie integration with civil rights, and labor was part of that. Organized labor can place the conversation of integration beyond the notion that white players will not want to play with Black players. The New York campaign had attracted college student newspapers, which began polling their readers about integrating Major League Baseball. In addition, more national sportswriters began to support the campaign. In Pittsburgh, labor issues had been a concern in discrimination in the steel mills for decades.

During World War II, the *Courier* kept up its pressure and criticism of Major League Baseball's color line. When the St. Louis Browns signed one-armed Pete Gray in 1945, the *Courier* commented, "the big leagues will take anybody rather than have a Negro in its ranks." That same year, New York City mayor Fiorello LaGuardia announced a probe into discrimination of the big leagues. On the heels of the mayor's move, Congress began hearings into discrimination in Major League Baseball. When pressed, Commissioner, A.B. "Happy" Chandler criticized Negro league owners for running a disorganized business, complete with gambling. He urged them to live up to major league rules and guidelines.

With pressure from fans, the press, Congress and New York City, Major League Baseball was prime to sign its first African American player. Branch Rickey took the initiative to sign Jackie Robinson to a minor league contract with the Brooklyn Dodgers' Montreal Royals in 1945. Rickey's choice of Robinson was based on his efforts to find a player with the talent, education, athletic reputation, veteran and disposition to face the racism, death threats and loneliness and keep moving forward. Jackie was a four-sport athlete at UCLA who, because of racism in pro football and basketball, chose to play in the Negro leagues for the Kansas City Monarchs.

The *Courier's* Wendell Smith, who began his campaign to integrate the major leagues seven years earlier, was assigned to Robinson, to not only report on his venture into white baseball but also to serve as a friend where none could be found. Robinson would eventually join the big team, the Brooklyn Dodgers, and sports in America would be changed forever.

Prior to Robinson's promotion, Smith forecasted the objections from other owners and even Jackie's eventual teammates on the Dodgers. On April 11, 1947, Jackie made his preseason debut and four days later his major league debut with the Dodgers against the Boston Braves. In the April 26, 1947 sports page, the *Courier* had a photographic display of the chronology of the *Courier*'s reporting of Jackie's debut.

While Wendell Smith was campaigning to integrate baseball beginning in 1937, Chester Washington was closely reporting and editorializing on the rising career of Joe Louis. Washington introduced Louis to *Courier* readers just seven months after his pro debut. In his column, Washington predicted, "New Heavyweight Hope Looms on Fistic Horizon." The column forecast a promising career based on a string of victories that demonstrated Louis's potential for greatness. By 1935, the *Courier* would feature Louis after nine fights in a cartoon montage. Advertised in the January 19, 1935 issue, sports editor Chester Washington and managing editor William "Bill" Nunn would present the "Life Story of Joe Louis" beginning on February 2. For the next fourteen years, the paper made Louis the focus of the sports section, except for the features on Jackie Robinson.

As Louis continued to knock out opponents, the *Courier* gradually made his rise a cause for crusade. At issue was not so much the integration of boxing—that had long been solved. The issue was whether Louis would receive a chance at the heavyweight title. After Jack Johnson's reign, the heavyweight division drew the color line for championship fights. Former contender Harry Wills predicted that Louis would not get a shot because of "the color line." The *Courier*'s campaign for Louis made sure he became a household name and that he deserved a shot at the title when the opportunity came.

Along the way, Louis was defeating all contenders. He destroyed former champ Primo Carnera in front of sixty thousand Yankee Stadium fans. He would fight former champs Max Bear, Max Schmeling and Jack Sharkey, with only the upset loss to Schmeling before his title shot. The Carnera bout marked the beginning of the politicizing of Louis's fights. The Ethiopian-Italian War was underway as Benito Mussolini sent in an Italian invasion force to the East African kingdom in 1936. The *Courier* covered the war with correspondents J.A. Rogers and P.L. Prattis. At the same time, Nazi Germany under dictator Adolf Hitler was increasing its military buildup under the guise of the "master race." This would have an impact on a possible Louis-Schmeling bout because of the racial politics of Nazi Germany and the fear that a Schmeling championship would draw another color line in the heavyweight division. In their first fight, on June 19, 1936, the top-ranked Louis lost via a twelve-round knockout to Schmeling, temporarily dashing any hopes of a Louis run at the champion, Jim Braddock. The June 27, 1936 front-page headline read, "Blackburn Blames Movies for Bomber's Stunning Defeat." There was no shortage of excuses for Louis's loss. Nearly all the *Courier* sportswriters commented on the loss. William Nunn wrote an open letter to Joe asking why he didn't follow trainer Blackburn's advice. Ira Lewis, the business manager of the paper, was given space in the sports section and asked, "Was Louis Doped?" But Chester Washington asserted, "Youth Still in His Corner." The paper added an extra sports page because of expansive coverage and opinion of the fight. Coverage, opinion and stories continued for a year as Louis climbed the comeback trail. Despite the defeat and Schmeling's protestations that he should receive a shot at the title, Louis would get his challenge to Braddock one year later, on June 22, 1937, at Comiskey Park in Chicago.

Louis had put the Schmeling defeat behind him. The issue for Braddock was that he could draw the color line the way all other white champions had since Jess Willard. But if he did draw the color line, it would mean that Braddock would have to defend his title against Max Schmeling, and many did not want the heavyweight championship in Nazi Germany's clutches.

Chester Washington kept a journalistic eye on boxing, and on Louis in particular. Washington did not have to campaign for integration the way Smith did for baseball. Politics surrounding boxing did that for him. Schmeling's protest of Louis getting a title shot before him would be settled when the confident German was given a chance to face Louis again. Washington, sports editor of the paper, and a team of *Courier* writers set up at Louis's training camp at Pompton Lakes, New Jersey. Washington was able to interview Louis after his workouts and sparring sessions. Louis told Ches, "I'm going to rub out that Schmeling smear this time." Louis was still "incensed" with the low blow delivered by Schmeling at the end of the fifth round in the first fight. Louis vowed that any Schmeling "techs" would be met with an alert fighter and that he was out to win. Schmeling was a German national whose rise as European champion and then world champion coincided with the rise of the National Socialist Party under Adolf Hitler. Louis's first loss to Schmeling in 1936 took place just two months before the start of the Berlin Olympic Games, as the Nazis wanted to give credence to Hitler's master race theory. But, just as Jesse Owens and his American teammates upset that notion at the Olympics, Louis would do the same in the second fight.

On June 22, 1938, Yankee Stadium in New York City welcomed a capacity crowd of seventy-two thousand. The gate for the event was $1,015,096.17. Louis would receive 40 percent and Schmeling 20 percent of the receipts. The lead-up to the fight played off the racial aspect of the match. Nazi Germany had already invaded Austria and was on the verge of invading Poland. Louis was put into the position of defending democracy, whether he agreed to or not. The irony is that democracy was not extended to African Americans, but Louis was expected to represent American democracy. Schmeling was not a card-carrying Nazi, although he was promoted as an example of the master race. By fight time, the crowd was very excited. Louis was a 3-1 favorite to win. The Louis that entered the ring for the second fight was steaming mad and could not wait until the opening bell.

The referee was Arthur Donovan, and he called the fighters to the center of the ring for the instructions. Louis bounded back to his corner and floated on his toes as he faced his opponent across the ring. At the sound of the bell, he proceeded aggressively toward his opponent. Schmeling was a counterpuncher, and before he knew it Louis was landing a hard measuring left jab to his face. Schmeling could scarcely get off a shot before Louis drove him into the ropes and proceeded to land left, right, left hard punches to his body and head. One right blast would rupture vertebrae in Schmeling's back. Louis eventually sent Schmeling to the canvas three times before Donovan and Schmeling's corner called an end to the fight at 2:04 of the first round. Joe was a machine that night. Black America celebrated another Louis triumph that was vicariously a triumph for them, too. Louis shattered the master race mantra of Nazi Germany and became a "credit to his race."

The June 25 edition of the paper had the broad headline on the front page, "Joe KO'S Max." Washington and Nunn had the front-page articles. Washington's lead article mentioned the fight as the shortest heavyweight championship bout in history. He mentioned "Joe Keeps His Promise" to knock out Schmeling; "Joe's Biggest Night" and "Joe Starts Out Jabbing" sublines recalled Washington's previous interviews and coverage of Louis leading up to the fight. Nunn's article was a recantation of the fight. There was limited radio in some poorer communities, so the newspaper was how people got the news of the fight. NBC Radio broadcast the fight, and it was live in Germany. Nunn's article offered a blow-by-blow account of the fight. In the sports section of this issue, guest articles by former champion Jack Johnson and former contender Harry Wills offered perspectives from the pugilist side. Johnson, the first African American champ whose reign ensured that no other African American would get a title shot until Joe Louis, offered his opinion of the fight. Johnson had picked Schmeling to win, and the first sentence of his article stated, "On the basis of what I saw tonight, I am forced to reverse my opinion about Joe Louis." Harry Wills spoke of the wonder of Louis and the prospect that it might be a long time before Louis loses a fight. He ended his column saying that Joe "has got the world in a jug." White America saw Joe as the foil for the Nazi regime in Europe. Just fourteen months after his triumph over Schmeling, Germany invaded Poland and World War II was under way.

As a champion, Louis would not draw the color line. His fifth title defense was against Pittsburgh-managed former light heavyweight champion John Henry Lewis in 1939. The fight would be the first in which two African Americans would vie for the heavyweight championship. In his entire career covering sixty-nine fights, Louis would fight eight Black fighters. He fought Omelio Agramonte and Jersey Joe Walcott twice. His fights with Ezzard Charles and Walcott came at the end of his career. His fight with Cleveland's Jimmy Bivins came during World War II, when Louis crowned Bivins as the "symbolic" champ during his enlistment in the U.S. Army.

The great example of local integration during Louis's reign as champ were his two defenses of the title against Pittsburgh boxer Billy Conn. Conn, "the Pittsburgh Kid," would have numerous fights with Black opponents. He fought "Honeyboy Jones" five times and Louis twice. His first two fights with Jones took place at Pittsburgh's Greenlee Field, home of the Pittsburgh Crawfords baseball team. Jones trained out of John Henry Lewis's gym in the Hill District.

By the time Louis's career closed in 1951, the civil rights movement had impacted the major sports in terms of integration on the playing field. The NFL integrated with Kenny Washington and Woody Strode joining the Los Angeles Rams in 1946. Jackie Robinson had integrated Major League Baseball in 1947. And Chuck Cooper had done the same for the NBA in 1950. During this decade, African American athletes would solidify themselves as invaluable if major sports franchises wanted to win games and attract fans. Boxing continued to move along as the color line faded away due to Joe Louis's long reign and the emergence of multiple contenders for the heavyweight crown.

The integration of sports in Pittsburgh and elsewhere certainly helped race relations in other facets of American life. The *Pittsburgh Courier* and its team of sportswriters and journalists helped open the doors for full participation in boxing and baseball. The principal journalists were Chester Washington and Wendell Smith. The team of writers and editors covering the first fifty years of the twentieth century ensured that integration would be a lasting part of sports.

Shown before the 1994 All-Star Game at Three Rivers Stadium is the unveiling of the Roberto Clemente statue. Today, the Clemente statue is one of four that stand outside of PNC Park, along with ones dedicated to Honus Wagner, Willie Stargell and Bill Mazeroski. *Courtesy of the Pittsburgh Pirates.*

BIBLIOGRAPHY

Newspapers

Chicago Tribune
Kenosha (WI) News
New York Post
New York Times
Philadelphia Daily News
Pittsburgh Courier
Pittsburgh Post-Gazette
Pittsburgh Press
Pittsburgh Sun Telegraph
Tribune Review (Pittsburgh, PA)

Magazines

NCAA Football Guide
The Sporting News
Sports Illustrated
Western Pennsylvania History Magazine

Websites

AZCentral.com
Baseball-Reference.com
Basketball-Reference.com
BlackFives.com
BleacherReport.com
BleedCubbieBlue.com
BoxRec.com
ESPN.com
GoDuquesne.com
GopherSports.com
GoPresidents.com
MLB.com
MSUSpartans.com
NFL.com
PittsburghPanthers.com
PittsburghPirates.com
PittsburghSteelers.com
ProFootballHoF.com
SABR.org
TheAthletic.com
TheRinger.com
Triblive.com
Undefeated.com

Media Guides

Duquesne University Basketball
Pittsburgh Steelers
Pittsburgh Pirates
University of Pittsburgh Basketball
University of Pittsburgh Football

Books

Buni, Andrew. *Robert L. Vann of the* Pittsburgh Courier*: Politics and Black Journalism*. Pittsburgh: University of Pittsburgh Press, 1974.

Finoli, David. *When Pitt Ruled the Gridiron*. Jefferson, NC: McFarland & Company, 2014.

———. *Pittsburgh's Greatest Athletes*. Charleston, SC: The History Press, 2018.

———. *Pittsburgh's Greatest Teams*. Charleston, SC: The History Press, 2017.

Finoli, David, and Bill Ranier. *The Pittsburgh Pirates Encyclopedia*. 2nd ed. N.p.: Sports Publishing Inc., 2015.

Finoli, David, and Chris Fletcher. *Steel City Gridirons*. Pittsburgh, PA: Towers Maguire Publishing, 2006.

Finoli, David, and Chuck Cooper III. *Breaking Barriers: The Chuck Cooper Story*. Seattle, WA: Amazon Publishing, 2020.

Finoli, David, and Robert Healy III. *Kings on the Bluff*. Seattle, WA: Createspace Press, 2017.

North, E. Lee, *Battling Indians, Panthers and Nittany Lions*. Conversion, DE: Daring Publishing Group, 1991.

Piascik, Andy. *Gridiron Gauntlet: The Story of the Men Who Integrated Pro Football in Their Own Words*. Lanham, MD: Taylor Trade Publications, 2009.

Peterson, Todd, ed. *The Negro Leagues Were Major Leagues*. Jefferson, NC: McFarland & Company, 2020.

Ruck, Rob *Sandlot Seasons*. Urbana: University of Illinois Press, 1993.

Robinson, James J., Jr. *They Call Me Jimmie Joe*. Seattle, WA. Createspace Publishing, 2016.

Legendary Pittsburgh Pirate Willie Stargell looks on following the final baseball game played at Three Rivers Stadium as the model for his statue that stands outside of PNC Park currently is displayed. Stargell sadly passed away the day PNC Park opened, on April 9, 2001. *Courtesy of the Pittsburgh Pirates.*

ABOUT THE AUTHORS

Having grown up in Greensburg, Pennsylvania, DAVID FINOLI is a passionate fan of western Pennsylvania sports, which has been the subject of most of the books he has produced. A graduate of the Duquesne University School of Journalism, where he is featured on the "Wall of Fame" in Duquesne's journalism and multimedia department, Finoli has penned thirty-five books that have highlighted the stories of the great franchises in this area, such as the Pirates, Penguins, Steelers, Duquesne basketball and Pitt football, to name a few. In one of his latest books, *Pittsburgh's Greatest Players,* he not only ranks the top fifty players in western Pennsylvania history but also includes a list of every Hall of Fame athlete who represented the area. Winner of *Pittsburgh Magazine*'s Best of the 'Burgh local author award for 2018, Finoli lives in Monroeville, Pennsylvania, with his wife, Vivian. He also has three children, Tony, Cara, Matt, his daughter in-laws Chynna and Susan, and three grandchildren, River, Emmy and Ellie.

TOM ROONEY had three stretches of duty at the Civic Arena. As an usher while matriculating across the way at Duquesne University, he worked at least one hundred events a year for four years (1969–73), a great way to see his beloved Penguins and actually get paid for it. For a decade (1981–90), he worked for the DeBartolo-owned Civic Arena Corporation, running and promoting events and marketing teams like the Pens, soccer Spirit and indoor football Gladiators. He spent four more years (1999–2003) working for Mario Lemieux as president of the Pens. Under the dome was his home away from home.

CHRIS FLETCHER, based in Forest Hills, Pennsylvania, is a writer, marketer, fundraiser and all-around swell guy. He is the former publisher and editor of *Pittsburgh Magazine*, where Chris won ten Golden Quill Awards. Under his direction, the magazine earned the prestigious White Award as the country's top city magazine in 1995 from the City and Regional Magazine Association. Fletcher also teamed up with David Finoli to author two other sports books, *Steel City Gridirons* and *The Steel City 500*. A 1984 graduate of Duquesne University's journalism program, Chris still dreams of catching one more contest in the old Civic Arena (provided it wouldn't be in one of the obstructed-view seats).

ROBERT EDWARD HEALY III, a Pittsburgh native, is a professor in the media department at Duquesne University, where he heads Duquesne's Sports Information and Media program. Prior to teaching, Robert worked as a sports information director and as a news reporter. In 2022, *Pittsburgh Magazine* honored Robert as one of its 40 Under 40 award winners. He and his daughters, Rhiannon and Josephine, live in Pittsburgh's South Hills area, where Robert is the president of the South Park Boxing Club.

DOUGLAS CAVANAUGH is a freelance writer living in Los Angeles. His most recent projects include collaborating on the book *Rooney-McGinley Boxing Club* with Art Rooney Jr. and his own book, *Pittsburgh Boxing: A Pictorial History*. He currently runs a popular Pittsburgh boxing history page on Facebook.

RICHARD BOYER grew up in the South Hills of Pittsburgh an avid sports and concert fan. He attended his first hockey game at the Igloo in 1969 and closed it out at the last concert. In between, as a Penguin season ticket holder, he experienced some of the greatest moments in Pittsburgh sports history. After graduating from Duquesne University in 1980, he spent his career in the insurance industry as an underwriter, account executive and now president of Exchange Underwriters, an independent insurance agency location in Washington, Pennsylvania. He is a director and senior vice-president of Community Bank and a chartered property and casualty underwriter, as well as a director with a minority ownership in Stoney's Brewing Company. Rich has always had a passion for writing and is grateful for the chance that Dave Finoli has given him to do so. Rich currently resides in the South Hills with his wife, Wendy, and two dogs, Sarah and Sallie. He has four children, Jason, Jessica, Joshua and Jennifer.

GARY KINN is a graduate of the Duquesne University journalism program, which he completed concurrently with David Finoli and Chris Fletcher. He has worked in commercial banking and real estate finance in the Philadelphia area since 1983. He has religiously followed professional baseball, hockey and boxing since 1970 and is an avid historian of all three sports. He has also attended more than one hundred live championship boxing cards in the United States, including in New York City, Atlantic City and Las Vegas. He lives in New Jersey and still believes that stolen bases are as exciting and important as home runs and strikeouts, that ties in hockey are an acceptable outcome and that there is only one world champion in boxing's eight weight-class divisions.

JOSH TAYLOR is a sports anchor and reporter with KDKA-TV in Pittsburgh, as well as a weekend sports talk radio host at 93.7 FM, "The Fan." A native of Pittsburgh, Josh was raised in the Hill District section of the city and is a graduate of Schenley High School and Duquesne University. He has won a Telly Award and two Associated Press awards for his work as a journalist and was honored as one of the *New Pittsburgh Courier*'s "Men of Excellence" in 2017. He is also featured on the "Wall of Fame" in Duquesne's Journalism and Multimedia Department.

A graduate of Duquesne University's School of Journalism, BILL RANIER is a lifelong Pittsburgh sports fan, particularly a fan of the Pirates. As an eleven-year-old, he attended the game when Roberto Clemente doubled for his 3,000[th] hit. Also as an eleven-year-old, he teared up when Bob Moose threw the wild pitch that ended the Pirates' World Series chances one month later. A much older Bill didn't cry when the ballclub lost to the Braves in 1992. He just told his guest Don Stape goodnight, shut off the TV and radio and asked God that he not blow up at one of his clients if someone brought up the game the next day. A native of Jeannette, Pennsylvania, Bill currently lives in Robinson Township with his wife, Marge, and daughters, Sarah and Meghan. He is the coauthor of *The Pittsburgh Pirates Encyclopedia*, *When the Bucs Won It All* and *When Cobb Met Wagner*.

SAMUEL W. BLACK is the director of the African American Program at the Senator John Heinz History Center. He is a former president of the Association of African American Museums (2011–16) and served on the Executive Council and the Advisory Council of the Association for the Study of African American Life & History (ASALH 2003–6) as well as the program committee of the American Alliance of Museums (2010–11). Black is a member of the Afro-American Historical & Genealogical Society of Pittsburgh and the former vice-president of the ASALH Dr. Edna B. McKenzie Branch. He serves on the board of directors of the International Black Business Museum, Pennsylvania Historical Association and the Sankofa Village of the Arts. He is the recipient of the Dr. John E. Fleming Award of the AAAM in 2016, a 2018 graduate of the Jekyll Island Management Institute of the Southeastern Museums Conference (SEMC) and a graduate of the 2019 Fulbright Germany Transatlantic Seminar of the Smithsonian Institution and Leibniz Association of Germany. Black is the curator of award-winning exhibitions and is the author of several essays, book reviews and narratives.

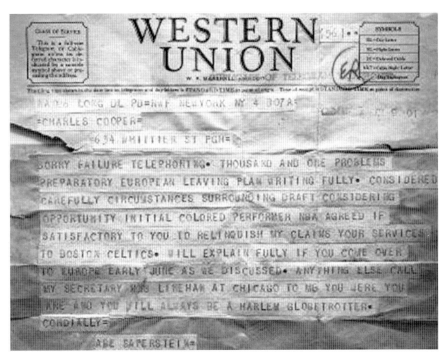

WESTERN UNION

NA046 LONG DL PD=NY NEWYORK NY 4 307A=

=CHARLES COOPER=

634 WHITTIER ST PGH=

SORRY FAILURE TELEPHONING• THOUSAND AND ONE PROBLEMS
PREPARATORY EUROPEAN LEAVING PLAN WRITING FULLY• CONSIDERED
CAREFULLY CIRCUMSTANCES SURROUNDING DRAFT CONSIDERING
OPPORTUNITY INITIAL COLORED PERFORMER NBA AGREED IF
SATISFACTORY TO YOU TO RELINQUISH MY CLAIMS YOUR SERVICES
TO BOSTON CELTICS• WILL EXPLAIN FULLY IF YOU COME OVER
TO EUROPE EARLY JUNE AS WE DISCUSSED• ANYTHING ELSE CALL
MY SECRETARY MRS LINEHAN AT CHICAGO TO ME WHERE YOU
ARE AND YOU WILL ALWAYS BE A HARLEM GLOBETROTTER•
CORDIALLY=

ABE SAPERSTEIN=

Shown here is the letter sent to Chuck Cooper by the Harlem Globetrotters' Abe Saperstien. It frees Cooper from his contract with the Globetrotters so that he could pursue his historic career in the NBA with the Celtics. *Courtesy of Duquesne University Athletics.*

Visit us at
www.historypress.com